According to Luke

*For the priests and people of St Francis Church,
Bournemouth, with many thanks for their help
and kindness*

According to Luke

A Gospel for a New Millennium

IVAN CLUTTERBUCK

First published in 2000
Reprinted 2003

Gracewing
2 Southern Avenue, Leominster
Herefordshire HR6 0QF

ISBN 0 85244 508 3

Typeset by Action Publishing Technology Ltd,
Gloucester GL1 5SR

CONTENTS

Publication of this work has been made
possible through the support of
The Society of SS Peter and Paul

AN INTRODUCTION

WHAT ABOUT THE INFRASTRUCTURE?

A daily newspaper has recently published a history of the churches, 'AD. Two Thousand Years of Christianity', in six weekly instalments. It is responsibly done by reliable editors and manages to give a mostly factual picture of what has happened to Christians over the last two millennia. Yet it is seriously flawed because it gives only one page to the teaching and ministry of Jesus and the first years of his followers. Perhaps this is predictable given the treatment the gospels have received over the last two centuries. A rising swell of critical scholarship which has been sceptical about the Lord's divinity, the authority of the revelation he brought, and the reliability of the gospel documents, has finally warned off ordinary citizens from entering this religious minefield. A leading article at Christmas 1998 by A. N. Wilson noted that there was a mysterious silence about material for the facts of Christ's life. There were no protests at this irresponsible statement. It is little wonder, therefore, that the gospels have all but disappeared from religious studies inside and outside schools. A teacher might well conclude that they are too hot to handle!

Such agnosticism about the person and teaching of Jesus is especially unfortunate when the ups and downs (and there were many) of Christianity over a long period are discussed, for it prevents us from explaining how progress could be measured against the original intentions of its founder. Were the seeds of later controversies to be found within gospel teaching itself? Was that teaching timeless and a recipe for spiritual needs in any age, or did it relate only to life in the Middle East in the first century AD? Was it a way of life only for individual salvation, or was it a life style for communities and nations? If we fail to answer these questions, we are unable to understand why divisions occurred among Christians and why a modern generation finds little in Christian teaching to help it with its aspirations and needs.

I believe a brighter day is dawning, and that we are at last able to take stock of New Testament scholarship and understand how much of it has been unproven speculation, and also to take another look at the infrastructure of the Christian faith. The idea that biblical criticism has overreached itself by failing to observe basic principles of research is now surfacing. In the last thirty years, some scholars, refusing to be put off by the jeers of liberals, have been producing a balanced approach which is uncovering details of the Lord's life which we thought never existed. There is some caution about knowing all the historical facts, but we can learn again what Jesus wanted for his Father's world and how he organized a following for its future proclamation. I have tried in this book to look again at the infrastructure of the Christian faith and to show that it has vital lessons for all generations.

We may approach our search in different ways. We may be happy with Luke's reason for writing his Gospel and accept that, like his historian predecessors, he has made a good job of collating available material about Jesus Christ, knowing that he would have been laughed out of court for inferior work in a very literate age, of which the letters of the younger Pliny in the first century AD are an example. There were, of course, limits in matters like geography, because a writer coming from another country would have been short of tourist information. But since the

gospel writers recognized that a vital element in evangelism and apologetic was the plain story of what happened
in the ministry of Jesus, they would have been anxious to
get as close to the facts as possible – 'that you may know,
that you may believe'.

If, however, some feel that solid material or hard fact is
unconvincing and that historians have to take probabili-
ties into account, as one scholar has said, they may be
helped by another kind of evidence. This can be found in
the results of the Lord's historical life. A few weeks after
his trial and death on the cross, a community appeared in
Jerusalem which had not been there before and which
offered a new dynamic way of life. This was based on
loving relationships, teaching, prayer and a distinctive
ritual of 'breaking of bread'. It attracted many new
members and quickly took root in other cities, including
Antioch, a few hundred miles north of Palestine. This
phenomenon may have persuaded Luke to explore its
genesis. He might also have been prompted by Paul's
post-resurrection faith which he was developing in
preaching and letters.

According to the book, the Acts of the Apostles, there
came into being a quality of daily life which had never
been seen before in a world which had mainly run out of
religious inspiration. This way of life, as Luke reports,
flowed from the teaching and wonderful works of Jesus,
first in Galilee, then in Jerusalem. If the thrust of the teaching was about loving and serving others, it was more than
a programme of ethical teaching. People were called to
make a radical change in their lives, a *conversatio morum* as
St Benedict was later to call it, not only for their own salvation but for the benefit of their community.

Since this change of heart was tied to the setting up on
earth of a true kingdom of God, Jesus may be said to
have engaged in politics, for a kingdom is concerned
with government, citizens and laws, and all these may
be seen in his teaching. We can see from the overall
picture of Luke's Gospel that Jesus organized a structure

of followers to support his ministry and carry it into the future. It was a form of politics in contrast and opposition to what was happening in Israel at that time, and which resulted eventually in the disaster of AD 70.

The way of life which was seen in Jerusalem and elsewhere after Pentecost, therefore, can be seen as a temporary consummation of Jesus' ministry which faded all too quickly. But where it has been recaptured in history, the Church has enjoyed golden days: where it has been forgotten, dark days have followed. Christianity has been described as being concerned with the transformation in Christ of personal relations. This happens when Christians first enter into a way of holiness and let it flow into the community round them. Personal piety is not enough in our modern world; it has to be distilled into the unhappy and violent world around us. This is a lesson which should be learnt from Luke's Gospel.

It would be wrong, however, to conclude that Jesus was concerned only with earthly well-being. He revealed what we could not discover ourselves, the nature of God, Father, Son and Holy Spirit, the Holy Trinity. Here we have three Persons working in harmony on behalf of creation and all creatures, especially mankind. They are perfect neighbours, living in love and mutual service, and willing the same kind of life for all men and women. It is this relationship which can be seen in all the teaching of Jesus, and when the first Christians followed this model, it could be said that the language of heaven was heard on earth.

This revelation was given at a price, for the power of evil or Satan was ever-present to obstruct the forming of the true kingdom of God. We see in Luke's Gospel the almost daily battle Jesus had with Satan. It is worth remembering that a life style of service to others can only be achieved when temptations to serve self have been overcome, and this means resisting evil. Jesus' fight against Satan has to be reproduced in the lives of all his followers.

Once the main theme of the gospel has been identified, we may note other special interests of Luke, the poor and outcast, sinners, women, prayer and the Holy Spirit, money and possession, forgiveness and a mission to all men. But these offshoots must not be allowed to obscure the overall message of the gospel, the setting up of the true kingdom of God in which all are involved.

It has not been my intention in this modest work to compete with larger and more detailed commentaries but to provide a guide to the latest balanced scholarship on this gospel. I hope to invite readers to study the whole gospel and not be satisfied with selected passages such as the Sermon on the Plain, the Good Samaritan, Prodigal Son parables and other much-quoted texts. Only when a gospel is read from start to finish can we understand the full implication of how Jesus preached and organized his kingdom. I have kept this book short for I know that many can be deterred by a large volume. I made this approach in my *Another Look At St John's Gospel*[1] and this has proved useful in both parishes and schools over the last ten years. So I have concentrated mostly on showing the progress of the kingdom of God which Jesus proclaimed. The Birth and Resurrection narratives have been allowed to speak for themselves. They provide crucial evidence for the bedrock of our faith.

I hope this book will be helpful for those engaged in religious studies, inside and outside school. It is certainly the approach I would make if I were back in the classroom. The ministry of Jesus forms the essential infrastructure for everyman's Christian faith and practice.

Ivan Clutterbuck

PROLOGUE

In the Bible, revelation is historically ascertainable and reaches its climax in the gospels. Yet the thrust of New Testament scholarship over the last two hundred years has been sceptical about their value for information about our Lord's ministry and teaching. Since the war little has been done to advance genuine historical work about Jesus. Rather has attention been focused on the early Christian faith and experience, in the belief that there, in a dubiously reconstructed Jesus, lay the key to any divine revelation that was presumed to have taken place in early Christianity (Tom Wright: *Jesus and the Victory of God*). This has led to a so-called mysterious silence about Jesus which the media has exploited.

Even traditional students have had to be content with looking for special features in each gospel. So Luke was seen to have an interest in women, prayer, the Holy Spirit, the poor and outcast and forgiveness. The overall scenario has been neglected.

The tide is now turning and a historical reconstruction of the Lord's life is taking place. This gives courage to explore the Jewish, and not the early Church, background to the gospels. Here we find that Jesus lived in an age of high tension among fellow Jews who were hell-bent on reviving past glories under David at the expense of any who got in their way. They believed that their God would support any ethnic cleansing that might be necessary.

Jesus taught that this was not the will of his Father in heaven, and promoted a kingdom which was based on love and peace, open to all peoples. Since the idea of a kingdom implies a ruler, citizens and laws, it may be said that Jesus introduced an alternative political programme in direct opposition to the Jewish leaders of the time. He failed and the Jewish nation headed for final disaster and the destruction of their most cherished symbols, forty years after the Lord's resurrection and the victory of God's kingdom.

Once we understand what was happening in Palestine in the first century, we may interpret afresh Jesus' teaching, not least in his parables. For example, the parable of the Prodigal Son becomes not a lesson on individual repentance and forgiveness but illustrates the religious situation of God's people. They had gone off into exile in a foreign land five hundred years before, having turned their back on their God and forfeited their inheritance. Now they were looking for a return. Jesus revealed a prodigal Father who was rushing to meet the exiles with a reckless love which exceeded the social conventions of the time. But Jesus was meeting opposition from those he was trying to save. The elder son represented this opposition. Despite this the father went ahead with his welcome and a great feast was held from which the older brother was excluded.

With this parable in mind we can, as it were, break the code of the whole of Luke's gospel. Only by entering the prodigal Father's kingdom may we turn aside from the violence and cruelties which nations wreak upon each other.

Luke's gospel has an urgent lesson for our modern times at the beginning of a new millennium. Despite the lessons of the past there is no abatement of the ambitions of some nations to revive glories of a past age at the expense of neighbours. Iraq and Serbia are the lastest examples of this, and we anxiously look round to see where the next threat will come from. Each threat in our times is potentially more dangerous because of modern sophisticated weapons. Only by understanding that there is an alternative solution in the teaching of Jesus about the kingdom of God, can we enter the new age with any confidence. For that reason Luke may be said to have written a gospel for a new millennium.

Ivan Clutterbuck
June 2000

THE BACKGROUND

A LESSON FROM THE PAST

Those who think that the present malaise of irreligion is peculiar to our modern age may be surprised to know 'both "honest doubt" and the spread of religious indifference were a constant source of anxiety throughout Victoria's reign',[2] according to David Newsome's survey of the Victorian world picture. He says that for the first time in English history the phenomenon of Unbelief emerged as so evident an intellectual and emotional problem that the whole question of what lay beyond one's life on earth, hardly ever before considered to be a matter of speculation or debate, became the subject of fierce and bitter dispute. This debate has continued to this present day and has become the more damaging because it has become a chronic condition, difficult to cure. Since, as we shall see, the thrust of criticism was aimed chiefly at the Bible and the revelation of God contained in it, it might be profitable to return to the causes of this major upset.

In the age of the Enlightenment, which started in the eighteenth century and continued into the next, many long-established ideas and beliefs were challenged and overturned, including and especially the authority of the Bible, which among other things had given the Christian world an explanation of creation and what followed. Now science showed that there was a more natural answer to mysteries which had puzzled mankind and this began to undermine the authority of the Bible.

Once this process started, no holds were barred and soon the New Testament and the person of Christ himself were put under the microscope. The work was chiefly done by German scholars, but their books soon reached England and started a line of speculation which has never stopped. In 1825 a German book, *Critical Essay on the Gospel of St Luke*[3] cast doubts on the historical accuracy of this Gospel and also questioned St Matthew's as well. Once the reliability of the Gospels was challenged, doubt began to spread about the truth of the miracles found there. The humanity of Jesus was stressed as opposed to his divinity, which in time was pronounced the creation of a later Christian generation.

All these doubts were compounded by the publication of Charles Darwin's *Origin of The Species* in 1859 which shattered the account of man's beginnings in the Book of Genesis. Such scholarship posed serious problems for the churches, first for men and women of intellectual standing, then for the clergy, and then for the nation at large. All this was very upsetting for an age which relied on the moral content of the Word of God in the Scriptures for setting a standard which would be more uplifting than that of the Georgian age. Men and women became not so much atheists as agnostics, and these free-thinkers began to develop their own morality which could be more demanding then the biblical code they rejected.

A further anxiety was uncertainty about life after death, heaven and hell, which had been so clearly delineated throughout the Bible. Hell-fire and eternal punishment found little place in the brave new world of the Enlightenment and thus vanished a powerful incentive for doing good and avoiding evil. This liberal wave of theology which swept in from Germany caught this country unprepared, and many were the clergy who longed for the good old days to return. There was, of course, another side to such controversy but the Anglican Church was not equipped to present it until later in the century. Since then there has been no shortage of scholars who have stressed that the Bible is essentially a religious manual and was never meant to be a compendium of scientific information. However, the damage had been done and there has remained in the common mind the idea that science has proved that the Scriptures are a flawed source of knowledge about the life and work of Jesus Christ. A Christian teacher who tries to convert the general public is liable to be faced with the old chestnut of science versus religion.

ET TU, BRUTE!

In fact, help from scientists in undermining the reliability of the Gospels is no longer needed because, since the last war especially, our own New Testament scholars have done the work for them. When Adrian Hastings (*A History of English Christianity 1920–90*)[4] reviewed the decades of the sixties and seventies he noted

> the ever-increasing scepticism which the leading theologians of the English academic school – Dennis Nineham, Maurice Wiles, John Hick, Geoffrey Lampe and others – were evincing in regard to all the central dogmas most characteristic of Christianity, the incarnation, the Trinity, even for some the very existence of God. It was most in evidence in relation to Christ.

He quotes Nineham as asking if it was worthwhile 'to attempt to trace the Christian's everchanging understanding of his relationship with God directly back to some identifiable element in the life, character and activity of Jesus of Nazareth?' In other words, if you want to know the will of God, rule out the teaching which Jesus, Son of God, brought.

Hastings sums up this unhappy era of New Testament theology:

Pleasing or displeasing, the consequence of their conclusions could hardly be other than the necessity of winding up historic Christianity, with a minimum of pain to all concerned, as unacceptable to the modern mind.

He notes that:

an agnostic world [was] amused to witness the white flag hoisted so enthusiastically above the long-beleaguered citadel of Christian belief, the stunned excitement of the rank and file of weary defenders on learning that their staff officers had so light-heartedly ratted on them.[5]

As we shall see, there is another side to the argument which is now holding the centre ground, but the influence of liberal thinkers of the seventies is still strong in the training of our clergy and laity. I have looked in vain at diocesan education courses for mention of the traditional scholarship which takes a more positive line on the reliability of our Gospels as sources of knowledge about the revelation of God which was shown in the earthly life of Jesus of Nazareth. If the old liberal ideas are not sounded out so loudly, they are wrapped up in a woolly outer garment! Scratch the surface of most bishops and clergy ordained since the sixties and you will find traces of the unsound and unproven theology which has been the order of the day in recent decades. As a very traditionalist bishop in Canada said to me after I had recently lectured on this subject, 'I guess there are some of those liberal views still under my skin'!

A SEVERED HEAD

All this is disastrous for the main ingredient of our faith, revelation. As Xavier-Dufour notes in his *Dictionary of*

Biblical Theology,[6] the religion of the Bible is founded on an historical revelation. This puts it in a different class from other religions, some of which have no revelation but rely on human intellectual experience of a philosopher or a transmission of revelation through a legendary or mythical founder – Islam probably excepted.

In the Bible, on the contrary, revelation is historically ascertainable. Belief for a Christian means acceptance of facts revealed in the New Testament by Christ, the revealer *par excellence,* which have come down to men through history. Once there is doubt about transmission, a church may be cut off from its head and this may lead to fictional material being inserted or even the fading of the original figure. This has happened in our time, as I have shown above. If the Gospels are not firsthand evidence for the ministry of Our Lord but secondhand opinions of a later generation, then we have the ingredients for eventual confusion and uncertainty.

There is, of course, another essential constituent for Christians, and that is the Jesus of faith who balances the Jesus of history. To leave out one at the expense of the other will lead in the end to a distorted spiritual life. It may also lead to teaching being attributed to Jesus which was never there. Over the centuries some Christians, especially Catholics, have been carried along by both liturgical and non-liturgical devotions, but this cannot go on for ever without the danger of producing inward-looking, individualistic people. The relationship which a Christian may develop with his Lord through prayer, Mass or visits to the Blessed Sacrament must be used within a community. We need to know how Jesus worked out his special relationship with his Father as he moved among his fellow citizens in a particular country, Palestine, and in a certain age, two thousand years ago. As Professor Moule has written, to accept Jesus as Lord without any historical information would not be about the man, Jesus, but only about an ideology or ideal – and this may well describe much of what passes for churchgoing today! As Moule says, we need to know what manner of man Jesus was and how he fitted in with the religious history of Israel. The alternatives offered in our Christian faith are not just mere history coupled with a rationalistic estimate of Jesus as a very good man, nor commitment to a preached but unauthenticated Lord. More than this is needed – an examination of his credentials as Lord and God, about his human character and the beginnings of Christian conviction.

Our gospel writers knew they had precious religious material in their hands. As Moule says, the Synoptic Gospels represent primarily the recognition that a vital element in evangelism is the plain story of what happened in the ministry of Jesus.[7] As we shall see, in St Luke's Gospel Jesus came proclaiming that his people's exile was over and that the kingdom of God was present in the world. His followers, who were clearly more numerous than just the Twelve, had to work out their faith in him by the way they ministered that kingdom to others. For this, Jesus provided a programme which can easily be understood by reading the Gospels.

GOD'S WAY WITH MEN

We may next ask why revelation is needed in our religion. The simple fact is that we believe in a transcendent God, beyond our comprehension and infinitely superior to the thoughts and speech of men. He is a hidden God, made even more inaccessible by the fact that through sin man lost familiarity with him. Man cannot discover for himself the purposes of God, and could well fall back defeated but for the fact that God takes the initiative and is the first to speak to him. Here we have a description of religion – God stretches out his hand to man who is struggling to come to terms with his existence. Without God's help, man might try to put together a good life but it would not satisfy his longing for the supernatural, for something more than a short life span. Throughout the Bible we find God revealing himself so that man may be able to meet him.

This was done through a chain of men called prophets, starting with Abraham and Moses, who were great leaders, and ending in the Old Testament with men such as Amos, Isaiah, Jeremiah and Ezekiel, who seem to have been a mixture of politician and holy man. All understood the Jewish vocation, given by God, to minister salvation to the rest of the world, and when in their later history the Jews neglected both their God and their calling, prophets tried to recall them to their duty. They warned of disasters which would follow unfaithfulness, but when these happened and Palestine was invaded and Jews went into exile in Babylon, they promised that God would not forsake them for ever.

All these prophets knew that they had been inspired by the one true God to stand out in front of their people (the meaning of 'prophet') and say unpopular things. But they also preached a loving, forgiving God who would never finally abandon his special people. It was this message which gave the Jews hope through the centuries before Christ when foreigners continued to occupy their land and their own rulers were corrupt.

So, God 'spoke by the prophets' as we say in our Creed, and although men such as Isaiah and Jeremiah were made to suffer by their own people because they said unpopular things, yet they were vindicated by events, and later generations both preserved their books and read them in their places of worship. They especially took strength from the message that God would one day end their exile and set up his own kingdom on earth. Into this expectation came the greatest prophet of all, Jesus. Just as in the past scribes had recorded the words of the prophets, so the prophet from Nazareth in Galilee had his following who not only listened to him but wrote down his teaching for posterity. Jesus indeed fulfilled what the Old Testament prophets had promised about a coming kingdom, but in a way which enabled God's chosen people to carry out their true vocation of ministry to all the nations of the world.

A VERY LITERATE AGE

More than four hundred years before the birth of Christ an important war was fought between the Athenians and the Spartans, the Peloponnesian War, and it was reported by an Athenian historian, Thucydides, who has been called the first war correspondent. At the beginning of his long work, he writes:

> As to the fact of the occurrences in the war, I have thought it my duty to give them, not as ascertained from any chance informant nor as seemed probable, but only after investigating with the greatest possible accuracy, in the case both of the events in which I myself participated and of those regarding which I got information from others.

He goes on to say what problems this caused, because people gave different accounts, out of partiality or lapses of memory.[8]

Dr Peter Jones, who has written a series on *The Classics in Translation*, notes, 'This passion for accuracy set the standard for all future historians.' Thucydides' influence in other areas too seems to be immense. He dismisses the histories of Herodotus, a near contemporary, as mere romance, but then Herodotus did not claim to be infallible.

Some may see an echo of Thucydides in the opening words of both St Luke's Gospel and his Acts of the Apostles. The conquests of Alexander the Great in the Middle East and beyond in the fourth century BC had carried Greek culture into many countries, including Palestine. The Jews saw this invasion of heathen customs as a threat to their religion and fought it fiercely. The books of the Maccabees in the Apocrypha tell the story of the Jewish resistance movement in the second century BC and its ultimate triumph, but this did not stop Hellenism from taking over many hearts and minds. Although the Greeks were no match for the Roman armies in 146 BC, it was said that defeated Greece in the end conquered Rome because the unimaginative Romans succumbed to Hellenist learning, and it became the custom for wealthy Romans to send their sons to Greek universities to complete their education. As far as the Jews were concerned later books in the Old Testament, especially the Wisdom literature, are largely influenced by Hellenist scholarship.

All this shows that the Palestine of Jesus' day was far from being a cultural backwater. Jesus and his disciples would have spoken not only Aramaic and Hebrew but also Greek and possibly a smattering of Latin. Matthew, as an employee of the Romans, would certainly have spoken their language and as a civil servant could well have had a knowledge of shorthand. We learn from Cicero (66 BC) that this skill was used in the Empire.

Luke tells us that Jesus took up a scroll and read it in a synagogue, and if we follow the first verses of the eighth chapter of St John's Gospel we are told that Jesus wrote on the ground. Incidentally, the Greek word *tekton* which is translated 'carpenter' also means 'builder', so the family of Jesus might not have been so impoverished as has been thought. Certainly the picture of a number of ignorant peasants passing on the gospel only by word of mouth is difficult to sustain when a closer look is taken at Jewish life in the first century AD. Preaching indeed there was, but no doubt supported by written material. St Paul's letters are full of references to the written word. From his Second Letter to Timothy (4:13) we can know that parchment notebooks (*membrana*) were used in Paul's circle.

With all this information taken from the text itself, we can revise the once commonly accepted theory that the Gospels were composed by a later generation who did their best to sort out material passed on by word of mouth, and edited it to reflect more mature needs and ideas. It has been suggested that the belief that Jesus was divine was part of this later reflection and did not belong to the original gospel. In support of this theory it was suggested that the miracle-stories about Jesus had been multiplied later.

Certainly, even before World War II I learnt that the writing down of Gospels was forced upon the early Christian community because 1) original eye-witnesses began to die out, and 2) Jesus did not return as expected. However, it is difficult to imagine even the first disciples allowing the previous revelation which their Master had given in his ministry to be found only on the lips of preachers. It is clear that Jesus did not just recruit individuals to follow him but trained small groups to put his teaching of the kingdom of God into practice. For this, some kind of written instructions would have been necessary when he had moved on to another town or village. As we shall see, teaching contained in the Sermon on the Mount was more than pious sentiment but was part of a programme for introducing a new-look kingdom of God.

WHY BOTHER WITH HISTORY?

David Newsome's book, *The Victorian World Picture*,[9] ends with a chapter, 'Looking Ahead', in which he shows how the Victorians faced the twentieth century. For a people who had seen so much progress in the half-century before, surprisingly they met it with sober reflection, and when Queen Victoria died this made them think even more deeply. There was a feeling that the country had been overtaken by change and the question What next? might well be asked. But they were still aware of their history, and Macaulay's *History of England*, together with similar studies, was very popular.

We may share today that Victorian apprehension as we approach a *fin de siècle* for, especially since the last war, we have been hurried forward on a flow of such great change that we are in danger of losing control of our future. It is at such a time that we need to keep hold of our history, otherwise we shall be like a man lost overboard who has lost sight of his home port and cannot see any destination ahead. Yet our age seems to have little interest in history, and the saying may well come true that 'the one thing people learn from history is that nobody learns anything from history', and this is a dangerous situation in which to be.

The Christian Church, more than all other areas of life, must never lose touch with its long history, otherwise it will rest only upon the spirit of the age, of the New Age perhaps. As I have noted earlier, the basic documents of Christianity have been so taken apart by critical scholars that their central figure, Jesus of Nazareth, has faded from general view. Just as there have been attempts in modern education to devalue our nation's history, so by a failure to teach the Gospels in and out of school, the Lord who came on earth to reveal God's purpose for us all can no longer be known, except through fictional presentations. It is a fact, of course, that if there is doubt about a famous person's life, there will be no shortage of attempts to fill the gaps. As I wrote at greater length in my book, *A Church In Miniature*,[10] Jesus has been portrayed in a guise which at times is insulting and which cannot be proved from evidence.

In an essay, 'The Revolution Theory from Reimarus to Brandon', in a book *Jesus and the Politics of His Day*, Ernst Bammel gives an account of the different roles Jesus has been invested with by New Testament scholars over the last two hundred years.[11] I give a list of some of them:

He was not divine – this was invented by his disciples
He was – a political messiah
   a social reformer
   an ideal who never existed
   a model for Marxism
   a failed teacher
   a failed revolutionary.

It is little wonder that the Victorians began to settle for a Jesus who was just a good moral teacher. In our day, Bishop David Jenkins and others have denied both the virgin birth and the resurrection. So our Church has been swept along a road of speculation about the exact life and work of Jesus Christ, and since the Gospels themselves are not being consulted in a professional and balanced method, the faithful are left confused, and this is an unsatisfactory state for those in search of a lively faith.

For most of Christian history the Church has not been troubled by destructive criticism and has accepted the Gospels as reliable records of the words and deeds of her Master, Jesus Christ. If some of her members could not read these records for themselves, they could at least hear them read in the liturgy and see them performed in the festivals of the Church's year, and could feel at Christmas and Epiphany, in Lent and Holy Week, in Eastertide and at the Ascension and Pentecost, that they were truly entering into events of the Lord's ministry. Without this faith, ceremonies would have become little more than folklore and distorted out of recognition. It has been left to modern times to lose the holy wonder of Christmas and to perform nativity plays with tongue in cheek. People may swarm to Midnight Mass out of habit or family custom, but the glorious triumph of Easter is largely neglected and Whitsun kept as a bank holiday only – sometimes. If there is no authentic script for the Church's occasions, why bother with them anyway?

RESCUE WORK

But a healthier age is dawning. Hastings notes at the end of his book on English Christianity that one aspect of a revived conservatism is a change in biblical studies seen in books, for example C.F.D. Moule's *The Origin of Christology, Suffering and Martyrdom in the New Testament* (edited by William Horbury and B. McNeil), and in a book quoted earlier, *Jesus and the Politics of his Time*. At the level of top New Testament scholarship, Hastings suggests a comparison could be made between the liberal views found in

Nineham's *St Mark* (1963) and Martin Hengel's *Studies in the Gospel of Mark* (1985) to understand how the tide is turning in favour of a traditional scholarship.[12]

Perhaps more surprising is the work of Bishop John Robinson, whose *Honest To God* threw alarm and anger into respectable church circles by its liberal theological suggestions. However, he had always excelled as a New Testament scholar, and in the mid-seventies shocked liberals by a book *Redating the New Testament*,[13] in which he showed that all the books of the New Testament were written prior to AD 70. As Hastings writes,

> His thesis in this book was an exaggerated one, nevertheless much of the argumentation was sound, and its conclusions could not but call into question a contemporary academic orthodoxy which dismissed the New Testament as highly unreliable evidence. For Robinson the New Testament was something still to be trusted.[14]

The same trust could be attributed to other scholars of the Cambridge school of Professor Moule.

Robinson went even further by tackling the Gospel of St John, whose historical value had been dismissed for many years as small. He showed that there were cogent reasons for accepting it as having been written very close to the original events of the Lord's life. I was in Cambridge about the time of its publication and saw the shaking of liberal heads at what they thought was the work of a naughty boy who delighted in adopting unpopular causes. However, it has never been answered convincingly, and caution has crept into statements that St John's Gospel is valuable chiefly as the meditation of a man in old age. I produced a simple version of Robinson's book, *Another Look At St John's Gospel* [15] (1990), and escaped being torn to pieces by the critics! If St John is early then we can build up a more complete picture of Our Lord's ministry.

More recently, Tom Wright has written a massive work, *Jesus and the Victory of God* (1966),[16] which directs attention away from a second-generation involvement with the composition of the Gospels which has preoccupied liberal scholars since the last war and focuses it firmly on their Jewish background. Using the latest information which is emerging about Palestinian beliefs and hopes in Our Lord's time, Wright shows we have to understand our Gospels from within the Judaism of that day and not from later Christian experience. He offers no new theories but points us back to what we already should know from Old Testament Scriptures. He suggests that Jesus did not come to found a new church, because he already belonged to one; rather did he come to reform the existing Jewish community from within so that it could respond to its true vocation – to bring all nations into the loving care of his Father, to be a light to lighten the Gentiles. Jesus' aim was the restoration of Israel around himself, beginning with the highly symbolic call of twelve disciples. Jesus intended to leave behind a community, a renewed Israel, that would continue his work.

As a reviewer in *The Tablet* notes:

Dr Wright passionately believes, and in this cause is ready to take on all comers, that in gospel studies history matters ... he claims that the overriding message of Jesus is not some timeless teaching on morality or spirituality, but his announcement, more often than not in symbols, riddles, acted parables and other coded language, of some impending great acts of God, to be realised through himself.

Since it seems to me that this approach is more likely than some of the liberal theories which have led to the scepticism of men like Nineham and others who have doubted whether we could have any definite information about Jesus, I have decided to adopt it in working over once again the Gospel of Luke. John Robinson started from the unfashionable and unpopular line that John's Gospel was early rather than late and followed it through the text, thus bringing new light to our understanding of the Lord's ministry. Wright has now struck out on his own and challenged those scholars who have played down the importance of history in the composition of the Gospels. By rooting these firmly in a Jewish background he has thrown fresh light on deeds and words, which so far has eluded students.

If we are surprised by the statement that Jesus did not come to start a new church but instead to restore a church which had been called into existence at the beginning of the Old Testament, we might conclude that the result was the same. Jesus created a reformed Israel of God which threw open its borders to all nations, and the beginning of this new era can be followed in Luke's second volume, the Acts of the Apostles.

If then we plan to return the Gospel of St Luke to its Jewish setting, it will be necessary to take a look at the Judaism of Our Lord's day and see how he fitted into it.

'Art thou he who should come or do we look for another?' asked John the Baptist. The answer was Yes, but was more demanding than the Jews had imagined. But then, God has always given his people a place in his plans.

THE EXPECTATION OF THE JEWS

To watch Jews at worship in a modern synagogue is to marvel both at an example of survival and also at a continuing pride of race. Despite more than two thousand years of persecution, holocausts and exile they retain a sense of superiority which can be seen in the assured way synagogue officials carry themselves. Ushers have almost a swagger as they show the congregation to their places. No doubt it is this pride which has infuriated nations who have had dealings with them.

Jews would trace their special place in the world to God's promise to Abraham that he would become a great and powerful nation and that all nations on earth would wish to be blessed as he is blessed (Genesis 18:18). This promise was followed later by God's revelation to Moses that 'All the earth is mine. You will be to me a kingdom of priests, my holy nation' (Exodus 19:6). Here was both a declaration of the Jews' privileged position in creation and also how it should be used for the benefit of all mankind. Their early history, celebrated vividly in Psalm 104, supported a belief that they enjoyed the special favour of the one, true God. For he brought them out of slavery in Egypt under Moses, led them through the wilderness and gave them the land of Canaan. Here in time they established a kingdom, first under David and then under Solomon: they built a temple where their God might dwell and lived under a Law which covered every area of daily life.

Then prosperity brought their downfall. The gap widened between rich and poor so that the latter were exploited by the former, heathen gods were worshipped and decadence took over. The book of Amos, who prophesied more than seven hundred years before Christ, gives a catalogue of the sins and wickedness of the people of God and is supported by other prophets such as Isaiah and Jeremiah. Although some kings tried to reverse the process, the nation was too far gone in its evil ways to be reformed, and disaster followed.

Instead of ministering knowledge of their one true God to surrounding nations, they had followed a programme of confrontation and were finally overwhelmed by more powerful armies. The Babylonians swept in, destroyed Jerusalem, including the sacred temple, and deported some of the Jews to Babylon. The last chapters of the Second Book of Chronicles described both the last days of Jerusalem and the causes of the catastrophe.

This might well have been the end of God's chosen people, but even in exile they clung to their identity by special ceremonies and by meeting together to read their Scriptures. The book of Daniel, written much later, gives interesting illustrations of how they survived heathen life in Babylon.

In time, a new foreign power allowed them to rebuild their city and temple, and they struggled to return to normal. But they were no longer their own masters and were ruled by outside powers, Persians, Greeks and finally Romans. To make matters worse, the priesthood which took over the rebuilt temple became corrupt and even compromised with the foreign rulers.

The belief that their God still had a great future for them persisted, and they looked for their exile to end and their conquerors to be destroyed. There were different ideas about how this would happen, but the careful keeping of the Law or Torah which they had inherited from the past figured largely in their hopes. In fact, to accelerate the coming of God's kingdom some Jews built a community at Qumran beside the Dead Sea where they kept the Law very strictly. Since the last war scrolls written by this community have been recovered, and it is possible to learn its expectations about the coming of God's kingdom on earth. Although a final clash between armies of light and darkness is envisaged, there is also mention of salvation by one man. We are told that John the Baptist left his father's house for the wilderness, and it is possible that he had some link with the Qumran monastery.

Other Jews sought to hasten the coming of the kingdom of God by violent means, and although Tacitus tells us that there was no open war in the Middle East during the time of Christ, there was a simmering revolt, likely to break out into armed conflict at any time. The unsettled situation in modern Israel where Arabs are in dispute with the Jewish government can give us some idea about the atmosphere in first-century Palestine. Without warning violence will flare up today and people will be killed, but now the boot is on the other foot because it is the Jews defending their authority and the Arabs seeking to overthrow it. Any leader who suggests a peaceful solution is unlikely to commend himself to hotheads, and so it was two thousand years ago. Meanwhile there are some citizens who look on with fear and alarm and pray for peace and quiet.

As Tom Wright says, the 'kingdom of God' was not a vague phrase and had nothing to do with what happens to human beings after they died. It was a Jewish way of talking about Israel's God becoming king. When this happened, the whole world would at last be put to rights. Meanwhile God was delaying for some reason putting into practice the plan that Israel knew he really had. The phrase 'kingdom of God' carried with it the hope that God would, within history, vindicate Israel. When he did this certain people were due for demotion, Caesar, Herod, and the existing high priestly clan. When God became king, the world would be ruled properly by rulers God approved of and they would administer justice for Israel and judgement on the nations.

The idea of God becoming king carried with it the dream of holy revolution. As Wright states, No king but God! was a slogan which fired the revolutionaries. It gave them courage to do the unthinkable: to tear down the eagle from outside the temple, or to assemble *en masse* to protest at the latest indignity threatened or inflicted by a heathen governor or emperor.

Jesus, therefore, came to a people who had high expectations for the future. When the kingdom of God came, the exile which they had endured for centuries would finally be ended, God would return to his temple which he had left, according to the prophet Ezekiel, at the time of the deportation to Babylon and he would rule there. Israel's enemies would be defeated.

Meanwhile they kept their hopes alive by obeying the Law as much as they were able. They had their sabbaths which reminded them that at the end of the present 'week' of Israel's story, there would be a coming day of rest when they would enjoy peace and prosperity. They kept their festivals, especially the Passover which reminded them of God's goodness to them in the past. So when a prophet appeared announcing that the kingdom of God was at hand he found an eager audience. We are told that crowds swarmed down to the wilderness near the Dead Sea when

John the Baptist started preaching. But, of course, he was only the forerunner of one greater who would outline a programme for a kingdom of God far different from the military aspirations of his people.

THE KING'S ANSWER

By the time Our Lord was born, therefore, his people were in a state of confrontation with the rest of the world. They had drawn a border round themselves and were prepared to defend it against all comers. The talk in Jesus' day was about military action against the Roman authority and about judgement for Gentiles and sinners. This was far from Isaiah's prophecy, 'I, the Lord, . . . will give thee as a covenant of the people, for a light of the Gentiles,' The lessons of the exile in Babylon had long been forgotten! There was never any future in taking on the might of the Roman Empire and Jesus saw that this would lead to disaster and ruin.

Instead he preached a loving Father who wished all men to be saved, and this conflicted with the Jewish belief in a God of vengeance. Jesus asserted the true nature of God which was found in the teachings of the prophets of the Old Testament. His programme could be seen in the Sermon on the Mount and the parallel teaching which is recorded vividly in St John's Gospel, especially in the final discourse at the Last Supper (chapters 13–16). Here he gives a command to love others and to live in peace. 'A new commandment I give you, that you love one another as I have loved you,' and 'Peace I leave with you, my peace I give you: not as the world gives, give I unto you.'

These gifts were not for a narrow circle but for the whole of his Father's creation. In his teaching on the good shepherd, Jesus says, 'And other sheep I have which are not of this fold: them also I must bring and they shall hear my voice: and there shall be one fold and one shepherd.'

All this was contrary to the expectation of first-century

Jews, which remained national, territorial and temple-centred. The Kingdom of God which Jesus brought knew no bounds, was open to all people, even sinners, and would only be achieved when the temple was finally destroyed. This brought Jesus into conflict with evil or Satan whom he saw as being responsible for the sad state of his people. Many centuries before, the writer of the Second Book of Chronicles had diagnosed the evil which had turned his people away from the true God and made them deaf to the 'messengers of God', resulting in the sack of Jerusalem and exile in Babylon. This evil one was still dominant and responsible for the exclusiveness of the Jews, which in the generation after Jesus' ministry would result in an even more catastrophic end to their city and temple. We see in the gospel narrative Jesus not only teaching love and kindness but also engaged in a life or death struggle with the power of evil, personified in Satan.

As we read between the lines of St Luke's Gospel we discover that Jesus did not go about throwing out good advice or *bon mots* to individual hearers, but organizing a small following of men and women who saw the folly of revolt against the powerful Roman authority, and wanted a way of reconciliation. For this supporting group he taught a way of life based upon the Beatitudes, the Lord's Prayer, and a loving ministry. There was to be a turning of the cheek and the serving of each other, even foreigners. He warned that this unpopular life style would end in suffering and even death, a carrying of the cross. So the gospel was more than a call to individual piety – the Lord's Prayer was a battle-cry as well as a bedside exercise. It was a call to mission. Twelve disciples were called, as most know, but also seventy (Luke 10) who after a training, no doubt, were sent round the towns and villages to prepare for the Lord's visit. They were to carry not weapons but a servant's manual, perhaps written down as aides-mémoire.

These events took place within a Jewish background about which we are learning more and more through sound modern scholarship. Jesus met opposition from his fellow citizens, and since he challenged the value of the Law and the temple in the coming Kingdom, he aroused such alarm that he was put to death. The resurrection proved him right and inspired his followers to take the good news to the whole world. It is necessary to assert the Jewish beginnings of the Gospels because, in post-war years especially, prevailing scholarship has placed their composition with a later generation who, it is said, moulded a mostly oral tradition to suit their spiritual needs. Since by then other nationalities were involved, it is strange that we end up with such a Jewish portrait of the Master! The symbolism and story-telling of Jesus make sense only within a Jewish scene.

I believe that when we read a complete Gospel we have a reliable record of what Jesus wanted us to know both about his 'Church' and our response to his love. The fact that the infrastructure of the Gospels is Jewish in character need not deter a modern generation from reading them and profiting from them. The theme of the Lord's ministry is the coming of God's kingdom and how his followers should behave within it. After almost two thousand years that kingdom still awaits adoption and fulfilment in our modern age, and the world languishes as a result. The evil one still keeps both nations and individuals in a state of confrontation and has to be resisted in the name of him who once wrestled to the death with him and won. The kingdom of God is based on co-operation, on love and peace, and must therefore be promoted in daily life if we are not to suffer a disaster greater than the Jews suffered in AD 70.

AUTHOR

In an earlier work (*A Church in Miniature*) I wrote that it is possible that the Gospels originally were headed only, 'the Gospel (good news) about Jesus Christ' and did not give the names of the authors. The writers were unimportant; the subject was all that mattered. In the ancient world an anonymous work, rather like an encyclopaedia today, implicitly claimed complete knowledge and reliability. As one critic has noted, the impact of the Gospel of Matthew could have been reduced if the author had written 'this is my version' rather than 'this is what Jesus said and did'. However, by AD 180 there were a number of books claiming to be gospels and the Church had to make a judgement about which were genuine. A certain amount of detective work reduced the number to four, which were attributed to Matthew, Mark, Luke and John.

Much discussion has centred round these names, but the one which emerges with any certainty is Luke. He is mentioned in St Paul's Letter to the Colossians (4:14) as Luke the beloved physician; again in the Letter to Philemon as a fellow labourer, and finally in the Second Letter to Timothy. In 2 Corinthians 8:18 there is mention of a brother 'whose praise is in the gospel throughout the churches' who may or may not be Luke. In his *Introduction to the New Testament*, Raymond Brown sums up Luke's credentials as follows:

AUTHOR BY TRADITIONAL (2ND CENTURY) ATTRIBUTION: Luke, a physician, the fellow worker and travelling companion of Paul. Less well attested: a Syrian from Antioch.

AUTHOR DETECTABLE FROM CONTENTS: An educated Greek-speaker and skilled writer who knew the Jewish Scriptures in Greek and who was not an eyewitness of Jesus' ministry. He drew on Mark and a collection of the saying of the Lord (Q), as well as some other available traditions, oral or written. Probably not raised a Jew, but perhaps a convert to Judaism before he became a Christian. Not a Palestinian.[17]

LOCALE INVOLVED: To churches affected directly or indirectly (through others) by Paul's mission. Serious proposals centre on areas in Greece or Syria.

After Luke's announcement about his purpose in writing, at the beginning of both his Gospel and the Acts of the Apostles we must take him seriously as a historian. As we learnt earlier, in the Greek world at least there was a long tradition of professional history writing and Luke states that he proposes to follow it. 'I, in my turn, your Excellency, as one who has gone over the whole course of events in detail, have decided to write a connected narrative for you, so as to give you authentic knowledge about the matter of which you have been informed.' We do not know who this 'Excellent Theophilus' was, and he might have been an ordinary believer, literally 'a friend or lover of God' but it is clear that Luke proposes to use all resources available to give a reliable account of all that the Lord said and did. Luke, therefore, would do his research among the many followers of Jesus – in addition to the Twelve there were the seventy who were also sent out to preach. Then, as he notes, there were others who had written accounts of 'the events which had happened' among whom was Mark whose Gospel might have been completed earlier than was once thought – and Mark had been on a missionary journey with Paul (Acts 12:25). There was also that hypothetical and enigmatic document labelled Q which, when reconstructed, consists of sayings and some parables with a minimum of narrative. The discovery of a Coptic document called the Gospel of Thomas shows that there were Christian collections of sayings. Luke's opening chapters indicate that he had access to information about Jesus' birth and childhood, to a collection of early hymns or canticles (Magnificat, Benedictus, Gloria in excelsis, Nunc Dimittis), and also to 1) a story of Jesus at the age of twelve; 2) a Davidic genealogy in circulation among Greek-speaking Jews; 3) a group of special parables, i.e. Good Samaritan, Prodigal Son, etc. 4) a group of miracles stories, e.g. Raising of Widow's Son, Ten Lepers, Catch of Fish.

This is some of the material Luke may have found. Since Luke is a very capable rewriter, it is difficult to decide how much material the evangelist composed himself. Luke created an orderly narrative out of all his resources and, as Raymond Brown suggests, has woven it into an epic sweep which begins with the temple in Jerusalem and ends in the imperial court in Rome, if you include the Acts of the Apostles.

Luke is a gifted story-teller, shown especially in the infancy narrative. Dante has called him also the 'scribe of the gentleness of Christ', and certainly he has given us a Lord full of forgiveness, with interest in the poor and outcast, women, and prayer.

DATE

As long as the liberal theory prevailed that the Gospels had been composed by a later generation who had added their own insights and spiritual experience, a well-advanced date, even into the second century AD, was possible. John's Gospel suffered in this way, and was reduced by some scholars to being a meditation on the Lord's life rather than serious history. In the 1970s Bishop John Robinson, however, took a different view and in a book, *Redating the New Testament*[18] claimed that most of the New Testament was written before the fall of Jerusalem in AD 70. He argued that this disaster was so earth-shaking for the Jewish people that any writing after this event was bound to show some trace of it, at least. And the Gospels, certainly, make no mention of it, but rather indicate that this catastrophe is in the future. As I said earlier, Robinson was treated indulgently by fellow academics, but gradually there has been some reluctant admission that he might have been right.

Luke shows signs of knowing Mark's Gospel, and if, as I said earlier, they had been fellow-missionaries this would have been natural. Much then depends on the date for Mark: if his Gospel was written after AD 70 then Luke would have been even later, 80 or after, but if Mark was early then we can look at a date round AD 65 for Luke. I believe this latter would have fitted in with the needs of an expanding Church. In fact, if Mark was even earlier – AD 46 has been suggested – then we have no problem with suggesting that Luke composed his Gospel when Paul's missionary journeys had ended and he was in Rome awaiting trial in the sixties.

I am surprised, therefore, to find Raymond Brown's definitive *Introduction to the New Testament* comes down on an AD 85 date for Luke,[19] although he suggests in another place that Luke mustered his facts to provide evidence for Paul's trial and adds 'give or take 5 or 10 years.'

PURPOSE IN WRITING

If today a new religion should set up business in a local community and begin to have considerable influence, we might feel that we should know more about its origins and beliefs. This is no idle speculation, because in our present religionless situation sects arise which try to inject their own life styles and tenets into what they see as promising territory. Jehovah's Witnesses, Mormons, Moonies and now New Age followers immediately come to mind. We might ask, How did they begin, What do they believe, and if they are good for the community.

St Luke might well have had these thoughts in the first century AD in Antioch, a city of half a million inhabitants, several hundreds of miles north of Palestine. There had come into this city a new way of life called Christian which was based on brotherly love and having all things in common, except wives. They also had their own rites of baptism and a special meal which commemorated the death and resurrection of their founder, Jesus Christ, who was rumoured to have been put to death under the Roman governor in Jerusalem. Luke's interest might have been compounded by the involvement of his friend Saul or Paul of Tarsus, who was not only a member of this way of life but was also gaining new members by his preaching and teaching. This was forcing him into difficult situations when hostile officials challenged this teaching.

All this gave reasons for Luke to research the origins of this Christian way of life and to use visits to Palestine to investigate its claims. There were writings which needed to be examined and eyewitnesses to be questioned. All this, no doubt, was necessary to help his friend Paul give a good account of himself in any investigations. There was also an overriding need for a work of authority as the Christian Church spread throughout Asia Minor and Greece. Professor Moule argues that all the four Gospels alike are evangelistic and apologetic in purpose[20] – to preach and explain. He suggests that Luke and John were written primarily for the outsider and Mark and Matthew for those already Christian. Luke would have been aware that, in a highly literate Greek world, careful scholarship was needed if his work was not to be laughed out of court.

Luke, then, is anxious to discover the details of the trial and execution of Jesus, for Roman justice was not only feared but also respected in the Mediterranean world. He is keen, also, to show that the Gospels are for all men. Simeon's song in 2:32 sets the tone with the words, 'a light to lighten the Gentiles' and elsewhere in his Gospel signs of a universal purpose can be seen. If there was agreement that Jesus' divine mission was to break down the narrow Jewish expectation of the kingdom of God so that all men might be saved, we may understand Luke's concern that this message should be implemented as the Church drove forward. We can trace three stages of salvation history in Luke/Acts:

The Gospel comes after the Law and the prophets because Jesus is loyal to Israel. In him secondly God has not changed the divine plan but fulfilled it.

Acts follows as the third stage because the Spirit who comes after the Lord's ascension gives the apostles a legitimate ministry to continue Jesus' proclamation of the kingdom. So the victory of God through Jesus is assured.

ST LUKE'S GOSPEL
(THE TEXT)

AN INVITATION

A historic house or building throws out a challenge for us to probe its secrets. It may well have been modernized but underneath remains evidence of past days, and we are invited to do research until we discover its origins. I occupied such a house a few years ago. It was part of an ancient foundation in Lichfield which had been built to provide hospitality for pilgrims in a bygone age. Outwardly the Master's House was typically Tudor but inwardly much alteration had taken place, not least by Georgian occupants. Old beams stretched throughout the house but they had been made to fit in with the plans of a series of later architects.

We might be tempted to settle for a house dated AD 1495, and there was good evidence for this year, but underneath the foundations were the remains of a much older building. It is possible to go down some old steps and enter a world within fifty years of the Norman conquest.

Even more interesting is the old church of San Clemente in Rome which still retains its mediaeval appearance, but which underneath leads to the remains of a first-century AD dwelling which may have belonged to St Clement himself. Even lower is evidence of pagan Mithraic worship belonging to a pre-Christian age.

Of greater importance still for us is the history of the
Christian Church of which all church buildings are mere
outward manifestations, and we do well to use the work of
historians to learn the faith and practice of the first Christians. Without a continuing link with them, modern
church life becomes rootless and ultimately meaningless.
But the final foundation of this Church is Our Lord Jesus
Christ, Son of God and revealer of his Father. Upon no
other foundation can our church life be built, and I believe
that through lack of knowledge about him our Christian
faith has floundered in modern times. In the past, Christians have learnt about their Lord from the Gospels, which
until modern times have been considered reliable guides.
But, as I have stated earlier, scholars have all but specu-
lated the person of Christ out of existence, and the Gospels
are mostly no longer studied inside or outside school.

I, therefore, invite you to take another look with me at
St Luke's Gospel and not to be content until we have truly
traced it back to its origins. We are seeking the truth of the
Gospel and truth in the Greek (*alētheia*) means taking a
cover off until we finally expose what lies beneath. It is
possible to strip off part of a covering without finishing
the job, but just as we are not satisfied until we have got to
the rock-bottom of an old building, so we must try to
penetrate the true origins of the Gospel. In the past, scholars have stopped short at a second-generation composition when mostly Greek church communities made use of
oral accounts of the ministry of Jesus, and produced works
which owed much to their own limited experience and
needs. If we start with this later Christian community (or
communities) we should be one leap too far ahead,
because the gospel of Our Lord Jesus Christ is essentially
a Jewish affair, and we must come to terms with Jewish
history and customs if we are to draw the utmost out of
the Lord's teaching. In this we have been helped in recent
years by a greater knowledge of Palestinian life in Jesus'
day through research by men like E.P. Sanders, and also
by the fact that Jewish scholars no longer live in a ghetto

and are willing to collaborate with their Christian counterparts. The results can be disturbing because we may be asking the unthinkable question, Was Jesus a Christian? and finding the answer is by no means certain. If the answer is No, we shall be in the company of some sound modern scholars. As one writer notes: in the twentieth century we have not been immune from creating Jesus in our own image. At the same time he writes that today we are in the fortunate position of being able to learn probably more about conditions in the time of Jesus than any generation since the first century, and in the light of such information we may conclude that in several respects Jesus was definitely not a Christian. For instance, being a Christian has historically meant not being a Jew and vice versa. The relationship might be seen as one of mutual exclusion and adversity and this can certainly not find its roots in the Gospel. Here Jesus is immersed in the task of returning his fellow countrymen to the vocation his Father had given them of being a holy people, to think their Creator's thoughts after him and to take that life style to the rest of the world. They were to set up conditions by which God could truly rule as king in all his world. The conditions the Son of God found on earth were adverse; darkness prevailed, his people were in exile and his mission was to bring such light as would enable his people to walk to freedom, as Moses had done centuries before when he led an enslaved people through the wilderness to a promised land. This mission occupied his short ministry, and apart from a few references to people beyond the narrow confines of Judaism, he could only prepare a small flock to break out into the light of the true kingdom of God where love and peace took the place of hate and confrontation. If we ask the question, Did Jesus intend to found a church? we might answer that Jesus already belonged to a church, and his work was not to cast it aside as useless but to mould and reform it so that it could serve a wider mission. Tom Wright says that if we see Jesus' aim as the restoration, in some sense, of Israel, beginning with the highly symbolic call of twelve disciples, then the apparently peculiar idea of Jesus 'founding' a community designed to outlast his death gives way to a more nuanced, and perfectly credible, first-century Jewish one: that of Jesus restoring the people of God, and doing so in some sense around himself. Anyone who cherished such a goal was *ipso facto* intending to leave behind a community, a renewed Israel, that would continue his work.[21]

If we are alarmed and confused by all this, words of Markus Bockmuehl may help.

And although Jesus was not a Christian, it is here we can identify ways in which Jesus is rightly regarded as the author of Christianity and stands in organic continuity with his followers to this day. He was a first-century Jew but several of his most central concerns have become key Christian concerns. This does not mean that they might not also be Jewish but merely they are of key importance to Christianity and can be shown to be in continuity with it.[22]

He goes on to list some of these concerns which include God's forgiveness of sinners and an intimate relationship with God as merciful Father as well as Lord. Jesus taught the acceptance of the weak, the afflicted and despised into the kingdom of God, and this interest he extended to include even Gentiles.

Such ideas and more are involved if we insist on discovering the true origins of our faith. If we feel, however, that our Lord's part in our salvation was smaller than we thought, we should remember that all the persons of the Holy Trinity were involved in our salvation, and if it was the Son's mission to restore Israel, it was the Holy Spirit who turned a limited and local phenomenon into a worldwide series of events.

Modern technology has accelerated the work of archae-
ologists round the world, and we have an ever-increasing
knowledge of the past. This includes biblical research, and
we are able to pass judgement on theories which were
held confidently: for example, the document Q, and also
Form Criticism. Luke's research was carried out from
closer quarters, perhaps twenty years after the gospel
events. He had contacts with both Jewish and Gentile
participants in an expanding Christian activity and could
understand the tension between those who wanted to
preserve the old Jewish identity and those who had a
wider vision. As a companion of Paul he would be on the
side of the latter, and would seek to make the most of
references in Our Lord's teaching about a mission to the
Gentiles. However, he does not forget the Jewish origins of
the gospel and makes this his beginning. This should be
our starting point too, and we should also remember that
Our Lord was not speaking *in the first place* to individuals
but to groups whom he wanted to bring into his campaign
on behalf of the true kingdom of God. As Wright suggests,
the evidence points to Jesus intending to establish, and
mostly succeeding in establishing, what might be called
cells of followers, mostly continuing to live in their own
towns and villages, who by their adoption of his way of
life, his way of being Israel, would be distinctive within
their local communities. It should be understood that
there were other kinds of groups, such as that of John the
Baptist for example. As Wright adds in another place, the
corporate meaning of the stories of Jesus did not undermine but actually enhances the personal meaning for
every single one of his hearers.

Luke, then, invites us all to make use of his 'treatise' so
that we may strengthen our faith, but it must be read as a
complete work and not taken piecemeal.

STATEMENT OF INTENT: CHAPTER 1:1–4

Luke starts his Gospel in classical style. We have already seen how Thucydides begins his history of the Peloponnesian War four hundred years earlier ... Herodotus announces that he wants to share with us what he has found out by inquiry, even though he cannot be sure of all his facts. 'Arms and the man I sing' begins the epic poem *The Aeneid* which describes Aeneas' journey from Troy to found Rome.

St John leaves his statement until the end of his Gospel when he writes, 'It is this same disciple who vouches for what is written here. He it is who wrote it and we know his testimony is true.'

So Luke declares his intention. Like John, he is writing to strengthen our faith, and we should believe them. I have heard it said in a lecture some years ago that they are making such bold assertions because they have something to hide! The New Testament writers knew that they had been entrusted with news beyond price, and were anxious to use it so that more might be gathered into the Church – there was no place for imposters!

A TALE OF SIMPLE COUNTRY FOLK: CHAPTER 1:5–25

Luke starts his narrative in a small village, seven kilometres north-west of Jerusalem in the hill country. Today it is called Ein Karem, and is much visited by pilgrims for it has no rival as the birthplace of John the Baptist. Zechariah lived here with his wife Elizabeth but they had no children. Zechariah was descended from Aaron and therefore belonged to the priestly family, entitled to officiate in the temple, assisted by a lower order of clergy, the Levites. It is reckoned that at this time there were as many as 20,000 priests and Levites, so although Zechariah lived, as we would say, at commuter distance from Jerusalem, he would have had few opportunities of carrying out his duties. Both priests and Levites were divided into courses and were chosen by lot to be on duty one week at a time. Some might even not be called upon at all, so when they were not serving in the temple they worked at other jobs, except farming, since the Bible forbade them to work the land. Some were professional scribes, but others might do manual labour. Herod employed some as stonemasons in the rebuilding of the temple. There was a restriction on whom they might marry, and one imagines marriage was kept within tribal limits. Most priests had no party affiliations but simply belonged to common Judaism. It was different with upper-class priests who engaged in politics and brought the priesthood into ill repute. We learn that some had their own hit squads to protect and forward their interests. Such politicking had so disgusted some priests that a hundred years or more before our period they had withdrawn to a monastery at Qumran in the bleak district round the Dead Sea where they tried to keep the Law very strictly.

Zechariah seems to have been dedicated to the worship of God, and we first meet him having been chosen by lot for the most coveted job of all – to enter the temple and burn incense. It is here that he has his vision of an angel who tells him that his wife will bear him a child. At first Zechariah shows disbelief. There is an echo here of the story about Abraham and Sarah in Genesis 17, where an angel announces to Abraham that his wife is to have a child in old age and he does not believe it.

So here we have at the beginning of this Gospel a reminder that we are still in the Old Testament among all the holy men and women who have waited for God to show his power and come among them. We shall remain in the Old Testament throughout the Lord's ministry, while he tries to recycle his people the Jews from a state of exclusiveness and revenge into one of love and welcome. Jesus is the bridge between the Old and New Testaments, and when his work is completed he will instruct his disciples who, under the guidance of the Spirit, will establish the Christian Church through their preaching and miracles.

Zechariah is struck dumb and, his duties completed, returns home.

There has been discussion about where Luke found the material for his first chapters. However, we learn in Acts 19 that Paul and his followers discovered at Ephesus disciples who still belonged to a sect of John the Baptist, and no doubt they would have preserved details of his early life. As for details about the birth of Jesus, it is clear from references in the Gospels that some of his family life at least was common knowledge (John 7:27; Luke 4:22). Few details escape village folk!

THE ANNUNCIATION: CHAPTER 1:26–38

The scene now moves about 70 miles to the north of Palestine for the beginning of the greatest drama of human history when 'the Word was made flesh and made his home among us'. From the earliest days of the Christian Church there have been attempts to oversimplify what happened when the Son of God was born of a young girl, Mary. Modern cultivated man especially has denied the virgin birth as being against nature and until recently has even queried the existence of the town of Nazareth in the time of Jesus. Certainly there seemed to be little evidence for it until excavations under the Church of the Annunciation in 1955 showed that the place was occupied before the Christian era, and an inscription from the Roman era, uncovered at Caesarea, mentions the name of Nazareth.

Orthodox Christian faith depends on the truth of the fact 'when we were sinners God sent his Son into the world' to share our human life, and chose a virgin to give birth to him. An age which finds little place for the supernatural has difficulty in accepting this fact. A modern theologian, Markus Bockmuehl, writes that 'the virginal conception of Jesus can be neither proved nor disproved.

For those who do not reject the possibility of miracle, Christian belief in the virgin birth is certainly compatible with what *can* be known from history.'[23] He acknowledges that historically the human birth of Jesus is shrouded in mystery.

Professor G.B. Caird notes that 'Luke certainly believed that he was dealing with real events, and it would be hypercriticism to doubt that behind these two chapters there is a substratum of the same sort of historical fact as we find described in a more down-to-earth manner in the rest of the Gospel'.[24] He also suggests that those who believe that the virgin birth is a matter of simple history must hold that the story ultimately came from Mary herself.

So the angel Gabriel announced to Mary that she was to be the mother of Jesus, the son of the Most High, and she in the best tradition of discipleship accepts the great privilege.

THE VISITATION: CHAPTER 1:39–56

Mary now hurried south to visit her cousin, Elizabeth, and this prompts the thought that she too might belong to a priestly family.

This is the occasion for the well-known canticle, the Magnificat, to be followed later by the Benedictus, the Gloria in excelsis and the Nunc Dimittis. All these seem to be a mosaic of Old Testament texts which Luke has woven into his narrative. The Magnificat for example seems to be based on Hannah's Song in 1 Samuel 2:1–10. Caird notes that, as in many of the Old Testament psalms the psalmist passes from his individual concerns to those of the nation for which he is the spokesman, so here Mary sings of her own exaltation from lowliness to greatness as typical of the new order which is to open out for the whole people of God through the coming of her son.[25]

We might regard these canticles as meditations or

reflections upon the great events which are happening, rather as we use responsorial psalms between readings at the Eucharist today.

If Mary went to Elizabeth in the sixth month of John's conception and stayed for three months she might well have been present at John's birth.

THE BIRTH OF THE BAPTIST: CHAPTER 1: 57–END.

A name to a Jew was important because it referred to the character and nature of the bearer. John was a shortened form of Jehohanan which meant 'God's gracious gift', and this summed up what both Zechariah and Elizabeth knew about their son (see John 1:6, 'there was a man sent from God').

When Zechariah was able to speak again he said 'God has visited his people', as a captain inspecting his troops. The phrase is used of God intervening for punishment or salvation. He will now also visit his people by sending a saviour, Jesus.

Horn of salvation (Revised version) means strength, so the phrase means a mighty saviour (Psalm 18:2). We are told that John was later in the wilderness until he was ready to appear before the public. 'Wilderness' would mean the area where the river Jordan flowed into the Dead Sea. The Qumran monastery of the Essenes was nearby, and it has been suggested that John had some contact with it.

THE WORD MADE FLESH: CHAPTER 2

There has been much debate over the words, 'the first registration when Quirinius was governor of Syria' because such a census in Judaea took place years later. However, the Greek word *protos* can mean *before* and this gives the translation 'before Quirinius became governor'.

Raymond Brown suggests that by associating Jesus' birth with the decree of Augustus Luke is placing it in a worldwide setting. The events described take place in a small town in Palestine, Bethlehem, but they have an importance both for the royal heritage of Israel and ultimately for the world empire. Brown writes:

> The announcement of the angels, 'To you this day there is born in the city of David a Saviour who is Messiah and Lord', is imitative of an imperial proclamation. If Augustus is portrayed in inscriptions as a great saviour and benefactor, Luke is portraying Jesus as an even greater one. This is an event on the cosmic stage, as the angelic multitude underlines by affirming glory to God in heaven and peace on earth.

Caird notes that 'heavenly host' sometimes denotes the stars (see Job 38:7, where the morning stars sang in chorus when God laid the cornerstone of the earth).

The Christmas story has been much overlaid with legend and local traditions but underneath it is possible to detect a simple narrative centred round three places, Nazareth, Jerusalem and Bethlehem. It may be that Nazareth is included because at some time Joseph went there to find work as a builder or carpenter – there was much building going on round the Sea of Galilee area and at nearby Sepphoris.

Two visits to the temple are mentioned in this chapter; one for the presentation of Jesus as a baby, and the other when he was twelve years old.

We learn from the former visit that his parents were faithful to the Law, and that two representatives of devout Jews waiting for the fulfilment of God's promises to Israel, Anna and Simeon, accepted Jesus. This is part of Luke's thesis that neither Jesus nor his ministry was contrary to Judaism.

Luke's account of Jesus in the temple when he was

twelve, in Raymond Brown's view, seems to have come from a different source from the other infancy material, and is more restrained than 'hidden life' stories in apocryphal gospels (e.g. Infancy Gospel of Thomas). Brown directs us to a persuasive christological sequence: In the annunciation an angel proclaims that Jesus is God's Son (1:35); at age twelve Jesus ... makes clear that God is his Father (2:49); at age thirty at the beginning of Jesus' public ministry God's own voice from heaven says, 'You are my beloved Son.'[26]

In this chapter, therefore, is the account of the greatest event in human history, the entrance of the Son of God into our life so that he might reveal to us what we could not discover for ourselves – the will of his Father. As John puts it, He pitched his tent among us (1:14; Greek *eskēnōsen*). In time this revelation will be made known to the Gentiles, but meanwhile Jesus turns his attention to his own people.

These first two chapters show that even if Luke was a Gentile historian he knew that the salvation which he had experienced was deeply rooted in the Jews and could be only understood in that way before it was translated into broader terms. With such travelling companions as Paul it could scarcely have been otherwise, for he never forgot his origins and argued from them.

PREPARATION FOR PUBLIC MINISTRY: CHAPTER 3:1—4:13.

John the Baptist.

Luke has already shown us how John will fit into the divine plan by being the forerunner of the Saviour, and here we learn how the Baptist's fiery tirade on the shore of the Dead Sea about repentance, about changed lives and widening the borders of the chosen people, prepares the way for the teaching about the New Israel which Jesus will give.

Luke is writing his Gospel for educated Romans and Greeks, and first once again sets events in a far corner of a great empire within imperial, national and high priestly reigns. Augustus Caesar had died in AD 14 after giving his people a golden age of peace and prosperity. He was succeeded by his son Tiberius, whose reign was not to be so trouble-free. We are therefore in about the year AD 29, although with different systems of dates, this must be approximate.

The word of God came to John as it had done to the prophets centuries before, and the scene of John's preaching was significant because it was on the edge of the wilderness through which under Moses they had travelled from slavery to the Promised Land, and where they had suffered great hardships. Some Jews looked back with nostalgia to those days because they were closest then to their God. The Feast of Tabernacles, in which they lived in tents, was kept every year and this reminded the nation of those days. Some rebel leaders took their followers down to this corner of Palestine and re-enacted Joshua's entry over Jordan as a symbolic gesture.

Now John stands up in the style of a prophet of old and calls his hearers to repentance. It is possible that this is winter because wealthy citizens would escape the cold weather in Jerusalem by going to the warmer resort beside the Dead Sea. He also is an agitator but calls not to arms but to changed relationships which will form the basis of the ministry of Jesus. John preached the coming of a new age and declared an amnesty for those who repented.

All this was done in a very sensitive political climate, and there were a number of hotheads who were ready to be provoked into military action. For this reason John would have been regarded with suspicion, and when he started attacking the morals of Herod he was arrested. Josephus tells us that the king was worried about John's growing influence with the people.

Unlike Mark, Luke rounds off the Baptist's story before beginning the account of Jesus' ministry.

The Baptism of Jesus.

John is not mentioned as baptizing his cousin but Luke takes the opportunity of mentioning two of his favourite themes. Jesus is praying and the Holy Spirit descends in bodily form – Luke's way of stressing reality.

At this point the genealogy of Jesus is given through Joseph back to Adam, the first man, thereby using another theme of God's care for all humanity. Here again Luke has his Gentile readers in mind, because he is anxious to show that although Jesus was the Son of God this did not mean that he was a demigod from pagan mythology, but a real man with a human family tree. So already in the early chapters of this Gospel we learn the two natures of Our Lord, God and man.

Our Lord's Temptations.

It is possible to see Luke continuing in an Old Testament vein, for he may well have had before him the example of David in 1 Samuel. Here the young man is anointed by the seer, Samuel, and goes out single-handed to fight Goliath who is threatening his people. So Jesus, having been baptized by John, enters into conflict with the enemy of God's people, Satan or the power of evil. There is no doubt that Jesus saw that the real enemy of his day was not Rome but Satan, and throughout the Gospel he constantly warns about the danger of the evil one.

For a modern generation, mention of Satan or the devil may not be taken seriously, yet few would deny that the power of evil is still very active and makes it impossible for individuals and nations to live happily together. Just as conflict has been settled in one place, it breaks out in another. Corruption and greed prevent good government, and people find it difficult to live at peace with each other – we despair of a settled world. It was the same in the time of Jesus, and had been for centuries. When the writer of 2 Chronicles 38 was describing the downfall of Jerusalem and exile in Babylon in 587 BC he was in no doubt that the wickedness and unfaithfulness of his people was the cause. They failed to learn their lesson and Jesus found his nation heading for disaster again. He saw that Satan was in control and was preventing the chosen people from keeping the covenant with their God. Therefore he must enter into battle with this enemy and defeat him.

Luke therefore puts the temptations of Jesus at the beginning of his ministry, so that his readers should understand that Jesus was not interested in personal power, profit or reputation. As Caird says, the devil 'attacked Jesus not at a point of weakness but at his greater strength – his compassion, his commitment, his faith.'[27]

Wright sums up the struggle of the Lord with Satan thus:

> What then must Jesus have thought was going on? How was the story working out? The battle he himself had to fight was with Satan, the satan who had made his home in Israel, and in her cherished national institutions and aspirations. The house had been occupied by seven other demons, worse than the first; so it would be with this generation. But, like Jezebel trying to seduce Jehu, the satan was attempting to lure Jesus himself into making the same mistake as Israel had done. If that turned out not to be possible, the satan would either try to scare him off, or to kill him ahead of time. If we examine Jesus' mindset from this point of view, a good many features of the gospel narratives fall into place.[28]

In another place Wright writes: David returns from his encounter (with Goliath) to a rapturous popular welcome and the jealousy of Saul; Jesus returns from his encounter (with Satan) to make what is in effect a messianic proclamation in Nazareth, as a result of which he is rejected by his fellow-townsmen, though welcomed enthusiastically by others. David eventually leaves the court to wander as a hunted fugitive with his band of followers: Jesus spends much of Luke's Gospel travelling with his band of followers, sometimes being warned of plots against his life.

Wright warns that this parallel is not the only or main key to Luke's Gospel, but shows that Luke is not simply collecting bits of tradition and stringing them together at random, nor writing against a background of events at the start of a second Christian generation. Rather he sees them as a climax to which Israel's history has been building all along.

MINISTRY IN GALILEE: CHAPTER 4:14—9:50.

Rejection at Nazareth: Chapters 4:14–30.

This is a longer version of Mark's account (6:1–6) and Brown suggests that Luke puts it here to explain why Jesus spent so much time at Capernaum. The synagogue incident is the sole gospel evidence that Jesus could read. He chooses a portion of Isaiah which refers to the Jubilee – amnesty for the poor which was part of the Jewish Law going back to Leviticus 25:10. This stated that every fifty years debts should be cancelled and people should be allowed to return to their ancestral property.

This meant a lot to poor citizens, and later at the start of the Jewish War of AD 66 the first thing rebels did was to burn the treasury where the records of debts were held. As Wright suggests, it was like destroying a bank's central computing system. Was Jesus suggesting that by announcing the arrival of the kingdom of God this meant a jubilee for the whole nation? Wright says that for several reasons this was not so. Jesus' use of Isaiah seems to suggest that he was using the Jubilee imagery rather than the Leviticus law itself. Certainly there was no further mention of this in his later teaching. Brown suggests that it was programmatic of what Jesus' ministry will be about.

According to Wright this could mean the kind of behaviour Jesus wanted from those who in the towns and villages were loyal to him and formed cells, groups or gatherings in the same way that non-Qumran Essenes, John's disciples and some Pharisee groups must have done. So Jesus did not expect everybody to keep a jubilee but intended that this was the principle by which his followers should live. He taught that they should forgive others not only their sins but also their debts, and this was the practice followed in the early Church.

Jesus, then, announced a new age, and at first was heard with joy, but when he centred this round himself there was anger that a local boy should take so much upon himself, and when he suggested that non-Jews should enjoy the benefits of the good news, this was too much, and they tried to throw him over the edge of the hill on which Nazareth was built. This fury of the people goes beyond Mark's account and perhaps prepares readers for the final suffering and death of Jesus.

A Synagogue was a place of worship and education and the centre of Jewish local life. It was controlled by elders and administered by an attendant or school teacher, who could invite anybody with enough learning to take part in a service. This incident then also shows the status and education of Jesus.

A question of identity; question and answer.

Chapter 4:31–7.

Jesus then goes north to Capernaum, a trading port on the edge of the Lake of Galilee, and makes this his headquarters. Here he teaches and performs miracles which leave people amazed at his authority. The first miracle brings him again in contact with Satan.

Chapter 4:38—5 end.

Luke says that Jesus proclaimed the gospel in the synagogues of Judaea but he may mean Galilee or 'the country of the Jews'. We also learn about Jesus' first meeting with fishermen on the Lake – note that in John's Gospel a first meeting with some had taken place where John the Baptist was preaching.

The geography.

With Capernaum as centre, the work of Jesus starts in earnest. We are told that he went out from there into towns and villages, healing and teaching. The names of some are known – Nain, Cana, Gergesa, Bethsaida, all lying within easy distance of the Sea of Galilee. Capernaum was a flourishing lakeside fishing port on the north side of the lake from which much of Palestine was supplied. There was even a pickling factory nearby and this would have been essential in hot weather. Interesting buildings are coming to light today, including possibly Peter's house. To the north was craggy hill country which was the border with Syria (the Golan Heights today). To the south and west stretched the plain of Jezreel which had been the scene of many a battle in the past. Here were towns and villages, among them a town which has recently been excavated (1983) and of some interest. This was Sepphoris, which even in our Lord's time had a chequered history. In 4 BC there was an uprising upon the death of Herod, and Varus, the Roman governor of Syria, burnt it down and sold the inhabitants into slavery even though they had nothing to do with the rebels. It was quickly rebuilt by Antipas and resettled and was known as the 'Ornament of Galilee'. Rich Galileans lived there, and there was an amphitheatre which has recently been discovered. It was a short way from Nazareth, which may have supplied the town with food and goods. It is possible that Jesus would have been there at some time and would have been aware at least of the Greek plays performed there – plays of Aeschylus, Sophocles, Euripides were high drama. Jesus used the word 'hypocrite' which is Greek for actor.

In these surroundings, a drama far greater than any Greek play was set in motion by Jesus, and all whom he encountered were called upon to take part in the action.

Who is this man?

At first there was little indication that high stakes were being played for, and that there was a race against time to head off the disaster which threatened the chosen people of God and which would overtake them within a generation. Jesus did not conduct a national campaign, but went from village to village in Galilee, gaining support and avoiding large centres of population.

First there were some healings in Capernaum, but since there were other holy men at work at the same time, Jesus might well have been mistaken for one of these. But as he continued it was possible to recognize that more was happening, perhaps even that the mighty works were signs of the long-awaited fulfilment of prophecy. As Wright notes, for the first-century Jew, most if not all the works of healing which form the bulk of Jesus' ministry could be seen as the restoration to membership in Israel of those who through sickness or whatever had been excluded as ritually unclean. He could be seen as a prophet, and would have been happy with this title, yet if he could name John the Baptist as 'more than a prophet', where did that leave him?

Jesus had his own programme which involved a private battle with the power of evil, and this showed him as having a special authority not seen before. This roused the opposition of the religious authorities, and his identity was questioned. When he began to speak in the name of God, to break the rule of the sabbath, to mix with publicans and sinners and to create twelve disciples (reminiscent of the twelve tribes of Israel) hostility grew fiercer.

The Twelve and others: Chapter 6:1–16.

Although the general public received Jesus with enthusiasm, reaction from religious authority was not so favourable. Jesus illustrated this opposition by comparing it with trying to put new wine into old skins (5:37) – it could not be done. At the same time he notes a conservative tendency of people who prefer old wine to new.

The time had come to organize the following which was building up round him into a team of disciples similar to that of John the Baptist. This latter clearly had its own discipline and life style and Jesus now began to build up his own distinctive method of promoting the Kingdom of God which he had announced. First, though, Luke describes the miraculous catch of fish on the Sea of Galilee and the amazement of the fishermen, some of whom would be the first members of an inner circle and who were to 'catch men' – the idea of mission is never far from this Gospel. Luke is the only writer to include this incident here, although John puts a similar event after the resurrection, and it has been suggested that this might be its proper place.

At this stage we might ask what made people follow Jesus apart from the unique authority which he seemed to have, especially over evil spirits. We could understand the war-weariness which comes upon a community after many years of living with the threat of violence. In modern times we have seen this in Israel, Sri Lanka and in Northern Ireland where there are periodic protests for peace against the men of aggression. Women especially live in daily fear for members of their family who might be the next to die in some scuffle or worse. The Jews had been at action stations for centuries, and there seemed to be no end to it. Some might well have been asking if God's purpose could not be carried forward without violence. The severe treatment given to the inhabitants of Sepphoris, mentioned earlier, thirty years before might have shown the uselessness of taking up arms against the powerful Roman military machine.

There was then an underlying reason for listening to teaching about an alternative kingdom of God, and we read that from early days there were some who braved popular opinion and gave it a trial. Later the parameters of this kingdom would be more definitely sketched, but at this stage some liked what they heard and formed groups in the towns and villages.

From these 'listeners' Jesus chose twelve disciples, and this was provocative in itself because there was that number of tribes of Israel and he could have been accused of setting up a rival 'church'. He was in fact trying to reconstitute the chosen people of God so that the kingdom he preached could be welcomed. We hear very little of most of the Twelve except for Peter, James and John. Wright points out that by choosing this number Jesus was following David, who had a bodyguard of three in his anointed–but–not–yet–enthroned king of Israel days. Earlier in the chapter (1–5) Jesus had taken David as an example when his disciples were accused of breaking the Sabbath. It should always be remembered that Jesus was acting within a Jewish symbolism.[29]

Note also that he spent the night in prayer before appointing the Twelve. Prayer is a constant theme in Luke's Gospel. Jesus now leaves the hills and returns to the plain where he finds a large concourse of people even from Jerusalem and Judaea and Tyre and Sidon. What follows is usually known as the Sermon on the Mount, but the area was and is gently-sloping terrain.

The Sermon on the Plain: Chapter 6:17–end.

The teaching contained in this sermon is widely known and has been used in different contexts to support moral conduct. But what was its significance historically and how did it fit in with the kingdom of God which was at hand?

We might read Wright's interpretation of the sermon.

[It] is not a mere miscellany of ethical instruction. It cannot be generalized into a set of suggestions, or even commands, on how to be 'good'. Nor can it be turned into a guide-map for how to go to 'heaven' after death. It is rather, as it stands, a challenge to Israel to *be* Israel. We may follow the main lines of the sermon and observe in outline the effect of reading it this way, as Jesus' retelling of his contemporaries' story.'[30]

In other words we should understand that it is directed at a particular point in Israel's history when its present unfortunate exile would be ended and it would be made manifest as God's favoured people.

1. Israel longs for God's kingdom to come and is prepared to work, struggle and fight to bring it in, but the people to whom it belongs are the poor in spirit, the powerless and not the powerful.
2. Caird notes that Jesus pronounces a blessing on those who have failed to find their satisfaction in prosperity, comfort, peace of mind and popularity. This does not mean that misfortune is good in itself. He writes,

It is only in the presence of a magnificent banquet that the hungry man is more blessed than the well-fed; and it is because Jesus has proclaimed the presence of the Kingdom that the advantage belongs to those who approach it with the greatest need and capacity for its inexhaustible riches, undistracted by the spurious consolations of the world.

3. Israel is weeping and wants consolation, but God will not give it the consolation of a national revival in which old wounds will be healed by inflicting wounds on others, but rather the consolation awaiting those in genuine grief.
4. Persecution will be certain for those who follow Jesus' way, but in the end they will be vindicated.
5. Israel wants justice, but this does not come by way of battles against physical enemies but through humility and gentleness.

If the Beatitudes are read in this way they can be seen to be guides for those who have chosen an unpopular, even unsocial way of life. Whereas at one time the promise of the kingdom would apply to those who were faithful to the Law, now it applies to those who are faithful to Jesus. This means difficult times ahead which many will not be able to face.

As Luke reports the words of Jesus about the uselessness of riches, he might have had in mind the sharing of worldly possessions which could be seen in the community in Jerusalem after Pentecost. Having described the kind of people needed for the Kingdom, Jesus continues by teaching how they should relate to others, even in a country under military occupation. In these conditions tit for tat killings become the order of the day, but Jesus says this must not be so. Enemies must be loved and served, resistance must not be offered, and generosity must be shown to all. The law of love, which John's Gospel describes even more explicitly, is to be the force which will govern those who follow Jesus, and this will divide them from their fellow Jews. Members of the kingdom of God must be different from others, and this is the only way daily life in any age can work. A story comes to mind of two Desert Fathers in the early centuries of the Christian Church. They had lived in the same cell for many years without the slightest disagreement. One said to the other, 'Let us have a quarrel as other men do.' But the other replied, 'I do not know how one makes a quarrel.' The first said, 'I will put a tile between us and say, "That is mine" and do thou say, "It is not thine but mine". So they set the tile between them and the first said, 'It is mine' and the second said, 'I hope it is mine'. The first said, 'It is not thine: it is mine'. To which the second replied, 'If it is thine, take it'. After which they could find no way of quarrelling. (Wadell - Desert Fathers) That was the spirit of the Sermon on the Plain and no doubt the spirit of the first Christian community in Jerusalem.

Wright asks, 'Did Jesus ... abandon the battle, and

preach a gospel of being kind to all people, with the element of fight and struggle taken out? Emphatically[31] not. The Jews of that day, and certainly Jesus, knew there was an alternative enemy who had to be fought. This was the dark power who through the years had masterminded attacks on the people of God. Six hundred years before, this spirit of evil had all but destroyed God's special race when they were overrun and many taken into exile in Babylon. As the writer of 2 Chronicles 36 shows, he had made them unfit to live with other peoples and even with themselves. This evil one had kept them in exile ever since, and Jesus saw his work to be to direct attention toward the real enemy: where he could be found, what his strategy was, and how he was to be defeated. Only then could the kingdom of God be established. Wright says we see this redefining of the real enemy prominent in the teaching of Jesus throughout the gospels, and certainly there are few pages which do not have mention of the battle with the power of evil. He notes that this theme is comparatively rare in other early Christian literature and is differently treated in non-Christian Jewish literature of the time. From Jesus' point of view, Israel could not identify Rome as the satan-figure and leave it at that. As we shall see, this theme is shown vividly in the Beelzebub controversy (11:14ff.) and the story of the exorcized unclean spirit (11:24ff.).

Rome indeed would continue to treat Israel badly – apart from the Varus incident at Sepphoris, between AD 26 and 36 in Pontius Pilate's governorship, there were at least seven other incidents. In the Sermon on the Plain/Mount, Jesus showed how members of his kingdom should behave in this age of great crisis and danger. He gave them what we might call a manual of instruction. This laid down rules for conduct toward both themselves and others. What appear to be unrelated sayings (6:37–end) are teachings about how a person's spiritual life should be disciplined so that the difficult task of loving others could become possible. The blind cannot lead the blind; a good tree produces good fruit and vice versa; attention must be given to one's own faults as well as to those of others. Above all, it is no good just admiring the fine sentiments of the Sermon: action must be taken, and taken from the sure foundation of the kingdom of God which Jesus was proclaiming.

We find deployed in this Sermon the technique of a great teacher. If most of his listeners found the going too difficult as the action shifted to Jerusalem, after Pentecost they were able to put into practice the hard lessons which he had taught. Meanwhile in Galilee they received enough instruction for first twelve, then seventy, to be sent out on the mission which Luke reports in a later chapter. Finally, it remains to be stated that the lessons of the Sermon are needed as much today as when it was first preached.

More miracles, questions, answers and mission: Chapter 7.

After this instruction of his followers Jesus returned to Capernaum where he was immediately in demand, this time by one who was not a Jew – there were Gentile sympathizers who admired the high religious standards of Judaism. It has been suggested that Luke included this incident because of the saying at the end that nowhere had Jesus found such faith as in this Gentile, but just as interesting is the fact that perhaps unwittingly the centurion had penetrated the mystery of Jesus' mission. As a military man he knew how authority worked by a chain of command. An officer could give orders but only if backed by a greater power, the emperor in the case of the Roman army. So he recognized that Jesus was performing miracles of healing because he was empowered from above. Hostile Jews attributed the power to the devil, as we shall see.

Jesus then went south to Nain where he saw a heart-rending sight of the burial of a widow's son. In what Professor Caird calls an act of love,[32] Jesus raised the dead man in the style of Elijah (1 Kings 17:23). Here we have the classic form of a miracle: a serious situation, the word of command, success and the effect on bystanders. At this point the difference between miracle and magic should be known: magic is done for the good of the performer, a miracle is for the benefit of another.

News of the Lord's ministry so far had reached John the Baptist, perhaps in prison, who was waiting for more dramatic action from the one he had heralded. Perhaps in the hope of the coming of the kingdom he had not hesitated to preach against the sins of those in high places, and now the opposition had closed in round him. There seemed little sign of the kingdom of God, and John began to have doubts whether he had backed the right man. Jesus replied by showing that all the signs of the new age were in place and that people must have faith.

Jesus commended the greatness of John who was carrying out his commission as ordered but yet fell short of understanding the nature of the kingdom. He still belonged to the old order.

In Jesus and John there were two opposite ways of life, one of austerity, the other of enjoyment of the good things of life. The Pharisees and lawyers had refused both – what did they want?

Chapter 7:36–end.

John, therefore, was not the kind of person you would invite to a meal, but Jesus was, and one Pharisee did so, even though he omitted the usual courtesies of hospitality, so important in the East. At least he called him 'Rabbi'.

The meal became the scene of an act of forgiveness which posed problems for the guests. The first was that a notorious woman should have the confidence to approach Jesus to carry out the welcoming formalities, and that Jesus did not avoid her but used her penitence to rehabilitate her in respectable society. According to Jewish religion, repentance and forgiveness meant going to the temple and offering sacrifice. Jesus offered this forgiveness on his own authority and by his own process, and this caused offence.

The preaching of repentance and forgiveness was an essential part of the ending of the exile and the coming of the kingdom of God. The fact that Jesus forgave sins should have been a sign that the kingdom had arrived and was available to all, but it seemed as if only the outcasts of society could recognize this fact.

Chapter 8:1–3 The women.

One of Luke's themes is the place of women in the gospel, and this is surprising for two reasons. He was a companion of Paul whose letters are full of anti-feminist sentiments. One thinks of such statements: A woman must be a learner, listening quietly and with due submission. I do not permit a woman to be a teacher nor must woman domineer over man; she should be quiet (1 Tim. 2.11ff.); or in 1 Cor.11:3. But I wish you to understand that while every man has Christ for his head, woman's head is man, as Christ's Head is God. In Titus 2:4 we find that women must be busy at home, respecting the authority of their own husbands. As Moule has noted, it is difficult not to feel that Paul himself is genuinely out of sympathy with the married state and generally his statements about the place of women in daily life puts him in conflict with modern feminism.

Then there is the tight hold Middle Eastern husbands have always kept on their wives. This was especially true of family life in Jesus' day which was admired by Greeks and Romans who had a lower standard. Women in the classical world had considerable independence and divorce was relatively easy, but this could not be said of Jewish women.

Yet in these verses we read that a number of women followed Jesus and provided for him and his disciples out of their own resources. One wonders what their husbands would have felt at their absence from home, and at housekeeping money being spent on other men! Professor

Moule tackles this situation in his book, *The Phenomenon of the New Testament*, and his words are worth quoting:

> It is difficult enough for anyone, even a consummate master of imaginative writing, to create a picture of a deeply pure, good person moving about in an impure environment, without making him a prig or a prude or a sort of 'plaster saint'. How is it that, through all the Gospel tradition without exception, there comes a remarkably firmly-drawn portrait of an attractive young man moving freely among women of all sorts, including the decidedly disreputable, without a trace of sentimentality, unnaturalness, or prudery, and yet, at every point, maintaining a simple integrity of character?

Moule asks whether this was due to the fact that the environments in which the traditions were preserved were favourable to such a portrait, but concludes that in view of the high morality of the early Christians this was not true. We are forced to the conclusion that this portrait of Jesus was just there and forced its way into the narrative. Jesus was not afraid of having the reputation of a wine-bibber and gluttonous man, of a keep of bad company, of consorting with women of dubious character. I quote Moule again:

> the extraordinary thing is that writers who must themselves have hated and feared the very risks they were describing and who themselves were not free from a repressive attitude, yet despite themselves, succeed in presenting a strangely convincing picture of Jesus – a young, unmarried man – allowing himself to be fondled and kissed by such women without either embarrassment or acquiescence in their morals.[33]

Jesus just accepts these women and their affection while moving them to repentance. It should be noted that the women were not all necessarily from poor families but included at least one from the royal household of Herod. Unlike the men, they followed Jesus to the very end and were found near the cross. Earlier it was suggested a peaceful coming of the kingdom was welcome to a war-weary land, and this would have been a vision women would have held on to as long as possible.

Chapter 8:4–15. The sower.

This parable has so much passed into the Christian and even general usage that we may be surprised to know that there is no agreement among scholars about what it origi-nally meant. We talk about words falling on stony ground, and this may mean not only in a religious sense. The preacher may know that his sermons may not always hit the target and can be wasted for a variety of reasons. Another lesson which has been learnt is that just as no farmer stops sowing because some of the seed is lost, so a preacher should not give up because he does not get a proper response. Such lessons are certainly contained within this parable, but we are warned by the words, 'if you have ears to hear, then hear' that there may be a deeper explanation.

Caird says that the parables of Jesus were not meant to convey ethical commonplaces, and Wright suggests that the parable should be seen in the context of Jesus' kingdom-announcement. So we have to look more deeply into the parable and recognize that it tells the story of Israel and the return from exile. Wright says that there is a parallel with Daniel 2 which concerns the kingdom of God and its triumph over the kingdoms of the world. In Daniel's vision a great image appeared of gold, silver and bronze, with legs of iron and clay. A stone hewn from a mountain shattered the image into fragments, and then grew and became a great mountain and filled the whole earth. There is a link here with Daniel 7 with its four king-doms and its 'Son of Man'. So, the unsuccessful sowings in the parable correspond to the failed kingdoms of this world which will be replaced finally by the successful kingdom of God which will fill the whole world. This may seem a fanciful interpretation today, but might have been seen differently in first-century Judaism which was waiting for a Messiah who would destroy foreign government.

Wright suggests that the same lesson could be seen in the parable of the wicked tenants (20:10ff.) where a series of servants are sent to look for fruit from a vineyard but fail. Finally the son is rejected but ultimately succeeds, for he is the stone in Psalm 118.22 which becomes 'the head of the corner'. So Jesus comes to sow good seed, but for different reasons it cannot take root. Satan, like the predatory birds, snatched the seed from the ground, or some preferred the barren ground of the wilderness. In the end the seed will succeed and produce a mighty harvest, but the opposition, those who expected to be in the kingdom, will not enjoy it. See the parable of the great banquet (14:15–24).[34]

If this was a possible explanation for Jews of Jesus' day, it might have been a problem for Christians in Luke's day, and so he brings the parable up to date (8:11–15). Yet the kingdom was still making its way through the world and had a varied reception. The sowing of the seed will result in a crop which defies thorns and briers.

Chapter 8:16–18.

A number of isolated texts follow the parable, the meaning of which is not clear. Verses 16 and 17 could be interpreted as Jesus saying the divine plan was being revealed at last. There had to be a time when this would happen, otherwise Israel's God would be like someone who kept a lamp permanently under the bed. V.18 'the man who has' may be the person who hears aright within the family of Jesus. 'He who has not' is outside the family.

Chapter 8:19–end.

Four miracle stories are now given, but before, (19–21), Jesus indicates that by preaching the kingdom and calling people to make a *conversatio morum* or change of life style, he is creating a new family relationship. Wright notes that this would be remarkable in any culture but in a peasant society where family relations provided identity itself this would have been shocking in the extreme. Jesus was now intending to make his followers to be a surrogate family and to sit lightly to membership of their natural family, even taking their children with them. They were to be a special group within the nation to live out the new life of the kingdom. Wright notes that in some of the Qumran scrolls the Dead Sea community members were to regard themselves as the 'true' house of Israel as against the 'existing' house of Israel.

All this is further proof that Jesus was not satisfied with a casual following but organized them into an efficient body, capable of doing their own mission work, as we shall see.

There follows a sequence of miracle stories, calming the sea, healing the Gerasene (Gadarene) maniac, raising Jairus' daughter, and on the way healing a woman with a debilitating haemorrhage.

Raymond Brown notes that these miracles are elaborate compared with some earlier ones, and show the grandeur of Jesus as he exercises power over the sea, demons, long-lasting illness and death itself.

Chapter 8: 22–5. The stilling of the storm.

It has been a liberal tendency to explain away such nature miracles and attribute them to a later generation who wanted to accentuate the Lord's divinity. One commentator says experienced sailors do not show that kind of panic at sea, and I can only conclude that she has not been at sea with hardened seamen in a storm! Anyway, not all the men in the boat were fishermen. With the great expectations which Jesus' followers were beginning to have of him, any such excitements and dangers were bound to have a special significance, especially after the crisis had passed. Sudden squalls or *shamals* spring up very suddenly on the Sea of Galilee, because the surrounding hills form a funnel through which gusts of winds can blow. My experience has been in the Persian Gulf where the same thing can happen. The sea suddenly rises and just as quickly subsides.

Chapter 8:26–39.

There follows a long account of the exorcism of the man on Gadarene or Gerasene land (the name is uncertain), which was Gentile territory. Wright comments that this incident illustrates the continuing battle which Jesus is having with the real enemy, Satan or the power of evil. He notes that all the details of this narrative are significant: it is Gentile land, the madman lives among tombs, herdsmen are nearby feeding the pigs, the demons are called legion. The situation is as unclean, from a Jewish point of view, as it could be. The indications are that Jesus is surrounded by places, people and influences that belong to the enemy of Israel's God. Jesus is fighting a battle against the enemies of his people. But Rome is not the enemy: it is Satan and his hordes, who are deceiving the Jews into thinking that Rome is the real enemy, and here is Jesus taking him on and sending him to defeat in the headlong rush of the pigs. As Wright says, it is a strange story, but this is what it might have meant at the time.

The end of this story is unexpected. Instead of being impressed by the cure of this madman who had possibly been a source of trouble for a long time, they asked Jesus to go away. It was all too much for them to understand![35]

In these verses 19–39, then, we can identify the *true* family and the *real* enemy.

Chapter 8:40–end. A double cure.

Jesus now returns to Capernaum and is welcomed, especially by Jairus, president of the synagogue, where no doubt he was allowed to teach. Jairus' daughter is very ill, and Jesus' help is sought. Luke follows Mark in combining two miracles. The woman who touched him had an issue of blood which made not only her but anything she sat on unclean, and this could well have barred her from normal society.

A Note on Miracles.

The word 'miracle' is used today to describe the works of Jesus, but the gospel writers refer to *paradoxa*, things one would not normally expect; *dunameis*, displays of power or authority; *thaumasia*, marvels or wonders: *terata* or *semeia*, signs or portents. As Wright points out, these words do not carry, as the English word 'miracle' sometimes does, overtones of invasion from another world, but indicate that something has happened within the natural world which we would not anticipate. Miracles as supernatural events have drawn two opposite responses within the modern Christian Church. There are those who have used them to prove the divinity of Jesus and therefore as a proof that Christianity is true, and others who hold that Jesus was a normal human being and that his later followers invested him with the role of wonder-worker.

In fact few serious historians today deny that Jesus performed cures. It is well-known that many ordinary men and women have through the ages found themselves able to heal people, given the right conditions. This power is certainly among us to this day, as this writer can testify.

It is important that miracles are not confused with magic, for they are very different matters. A miracle has to do with the gracious act of a god, while magic is all about human manipulation of divine or quasi-divine forces. Jesus certainly did not dabble in magic, although his enemies might have accused him of doing so, and we need to tone down the idea that he performed miracles as such.

How then did Jesus see his wonderful cures and works? Certainly he did not do them to impress or gain popularity, for we find him trying to escape from the enthusiasm his works caused. He used them to prove that the kingdom of God had broken in to his people, that a new

age had come which had been promised by the prophets
centuries before.

> Here is your God.
> He will come with vengeance with terrible recompense.
> He will come and save you.
> Then the eyes of the blind will be opened and the ears of
> the deaf unstopped;
> then the lame shall leap like a deer and the tongue of the
> speechless sing for joy (Isaiah 35).

There is also a Qumran text which runs like this:

> for the heavens and the earth will listen to his Messiah
> ... For he will honour the devout upon the throne of
> eternal royalty, freeing prisoners, giving sight to the
> blind ... he will make the dead alive, he will proclaim
> good news to the meek, give lavishly to the needy, lead
> the exiled and enrich the hungry.

As we have seen earlier, Jesus saw his vocation as fighting the power of evil, saving his people from the grip of
Satan, and each mighty work was the pushing back of evil
forces. He could say, 'If it is by the finger of God that I
drive out the devils, then be sure the kingdom of God has
already come upon you.' The ending of exile and the
coming of the kingdom in the person of Jesus worked even
more widely because its arrival was an open welcome to
those who had been barred from being full members of the
worshipping community, the blind, the deaf, lepers, the
ritually unclean, the crippled, and also Gentiles and
Samaritans for whom Jesus performed miracles. This
undermined the Jewish *status quo* and was to get him into
trouble, but for him it was an essential accompaniment to
the new order he was inaugurating.

Whether or not the cured saw it in this way is not
known, but one blind man could follow Jesus in the way
(Mark 10:52). Some no doubt were just grateful, but others

might have joined those who already were forming the new group of followers. All these would see unexplained happenings such as a stilling of a storm or the feeding of a large number of people as further evidence of the Master's authority and power.

Raymond Brown has an interesting comment on those who accept the healings of Jesus but reject the historicity of 'nature' miracles. He says that

> that distinction finds no support in an OT background where God manifests power over all creation. Just as sickness and affliction reflect the kingdom of evil, so also does a dangerous storm; accordingly Jesus rebukes the wind and the sea just as he does a demon. (Lest one thinks this picture impossibly naive, one should note that when a storm causes death and destruction today, people wonder why God has allowed this; they do not vent their anger on a high pressure system.) The victory of Jesus over the storm is seen as the action of the stronger one whom even the wind and sea obey.[36]

It can also be noted that whereas the touching of dead bodies like that of Jairus' daughter should have brought Jesus uncleanness, instead it brought a restoration to life, and this is another example of his power.

The Organization of the Kingdom: Chapters 9:1–17 and 10:1–12.

I have put these verses together because they are all concerned with the organization and management of the kingdom which Jesus was preaching. This subject may surprise today's Christian who uses the gospels to feed his religious life by selecting a few well-chosen passages, such as the Sermon on the Mount, the Good Samaritan and the command to love etc., and never sees the full scenario. He/she is like a person putting his fingers into a fruit pie and pulling out a few juicy plums without seeing what the whole pie is made of as well. He is happy to go along with those scholars who have taught that a second or third generation of early Christians composed the Gospels by selecting from oral traditions those parts which fitted in with their spiritual needs and experience.

It may be a shock, therefore, to go further back to the true origins of the Gospel and learn what Our Lord's ministry meant to his own compatriots. This can only be understood by taking each Gospel as a whole. It is then that we begin to realize the political implications of the preaching of the kingdom of God. A kingdom must of necessity have a king, it must have rules and also recognize who should be its citizens. On all of these three fundamentals Jesus clashed violently with the authorities of his time. For he saw himself as the king, although not in the way the world saw kingship; he rewrote the Law or Torah as a way of life, and he opened his kingdom to those who were being excluded, foreigners, outcasts and sinners. It was inevitable, therefore, that he should incur the hostility of the Establishment. As Tom Wright writes,

> Anyone announcing the kingdom of YHWH was engaging in serious political action. Anyone announcing the kingdom *but explicitly opposing armed resistance* was engaging in doubly serious political action: not only the occupying forces, but all those who gave allegiance to the resistance movement, would be enraged.[37]

Wright goes on to say that since some of the most ardent revolutionaries were hard-line Pharisees this helps to explain the real nature of Jesus' controversies with them. It also explains the interest shown in the movement by Herod. He had executed John the Baptist who had stirred up unrest, but now he found another had appeared in his place. Only perhaps when a convicted Jesus was sent to him before his crucifixion could Herod be persuaded that here was no dangerous rival.

There were a certain number of ordinary Jews who, as

we have seen, liked what Jesus was saying, and these Jesus gathered together and trained. All Jesus' hearers were summoned to take part in the action and to live as members of the kingdom. Jesus called at least some of these hearers not only to be loyal to him and his movement but to leave their homes and follow him. As Wright says, 'He had an agenda, a purpose he was eager to accomplish. For this, he needed associates, and even helpers'. Today we would call them activists, and these people have to be trained.

So Jesus was also involved in a social revolution since (Wright) 'to persuade even small groups within the villages to change their behaviour to the extent just outlined represented a serious challenge to existing practices'. Wright suggests that a passage in Matthew 18:15–18, which gives directions for regulating relationships between 'brothers', might well illustrate a situation which could have arisen within Our Lord's own ministry, and not have been the creation of the later church.

Jesus' revolution was theological. In the place of the contemporary Jewish God who was enclosed within a land, a Law and a temple and was also committed to vengeance on Gentile oppressors, he believed in a God of love, grace and mercy, as shown in the Old Testament and especially in the prophet Isaiah:

> These are the words of the Lord who is God,
> who created the heavens and stretched them out,
> who fashioned the earth
> and everything that grows in it,
> giving breath to its people
> and life to those who walk on it:
> I the Lord have called you with righteous purpose
> and taken you by the hand;
> I have formed you, and destined you
> to be a light for peoples,
> a lamp for nations . . . (42:5,6)

A mission to the Gentiles is foreshadowed at the very beginning of Israel's history when Abraham was called (Genesis 12:3), and later when, after the exodus from Egypt, God tells Moses that the sons of Israel will be a kingdom of priests and ministers to all the nations on the earth (Exodus 19:5,6). Jesus returned his people to this true God at a time when those ideas were very unpopular among the Jews.

Jesus' revolution was theological also because it called into existence cells of followers committed to his way of life. As Wright writes,

> Jesus, like the founder(s) of the Essenes, and like John the Baptist, apparently envisaged that, scattered about Palestine, there would be small groups of people loyal to himself, who would get together to encourage one another, and would act as members of a family, sharing some sort of common life and, in particular, exercising mutual forgiveness. It was because this way of life was what it was, while reflecting the theology it did, that Jesus' whole movement was thoroughly, and dangerously, 'political'.[38]

With all this in mind we are ready to return to the verses in Luke, chapters 9 and 10, which we are considering. The Twelve were the first to be called and the first, therefore, to be trained in a mission of preaching and healing. This escalation no doubt worried Herod. Luke does not relate the story of the Baptist's beheading, but leaves it to be implied in Herod's question about the identity of Jesus.

If the Twelve had been trained in a small group, now was the time for an even greater mission, and so we are taken to a remote spot near Bethsaida (9:10). The Aramaic for this town means 'house of fishing' and it was in fact on the northern edge of the Lake of Galilee and on the border with Ituraea. It was the home of Peter, Andrew and Philip, according to John 1:44. It was one of the towns cursed by Jesus (Luke 10:13) and that may be the reason why Jesus had to retire to a remote place for the day's instruction. There we are told he taught them about the kingdom of God. He also healed some, and this no doubt bound his followers even more closely to him.

Chapters 9:11. He spoke to them about the kingdom of God.

The feeding of a large number of people in an isolated place has attracted so much attention that we pass lightly over the reason for the crowd being there at all. In fact the extraordinary feat of providing a spontaneous picnic attracts no comment at all in the first three Gospels, and in St John the people see it as a sign that a prophet has come into the world. The crowd in Luke's Gospel might have said 'and more than a prophet' because Jesus is about to be recognized as the Messiah (v.20). The provision of a Messianic banquet was part of the programme of the kingdom of God, and so the feeding of the five thousand might be seen as further proof that in Jesus a new age had come.

This should not distract us from recognizing the main business of the day, which was instruction in the kingdom of God. Since Jesus would have repeated his teaching many times we can gather from the Gospels generally what he said on this day near Bethsaida. He would certainly have called for that 'renewal of heart' demanded in the book of Deuteronomy and preached by Jeremiah and Ezekiel. There would have been a call to go behind the Law to its very centre where love of God and neighbour is commanded, for without this renewal of heart the kingdom which Jesus preached could not go forward. No doubt Jesus would have wanted to bring all his followers to that statement by a scribe in Mark 12:32–34 who said, 'You are right in saying that God is one and beside him there is no other. And to love him with all your heart, all your understanding and all your strength and to love your neighbour as yourself means more than any burnt offerings and sacrifices'. Jesus commended him by saying that he was not far from the kingdom of God.

To such a point Jesus would have wanted to bring the large crowd of followers who listened to his instruction in a desert place, because from these people he would soon choose seventy or more and send them into the towns and villages in Galilee and possibly further south. The conference over, the members had to be fed and this Jesus did in a wonderful way.

Chapter 9:18–27. The confession of Peter.

These verses should not be taken separately from what has gone before. A teacher has to be certain that his pupils recognize his authority and qualifications to teach, and so here we have a profession of faith that the disciples' leader is greater than John the Baptist or any of the old prophets. With this lesson learnt Jesus can warn them about the unpleasant part, that following his way of life would lead to suffering. We have already noted that Jesus was on a head-on collision course with the political leaders of his day. They were interested only in gaining the whole world, but it was a way which would lead to destruction. At this stage, few of Our Lord's followers would have been able to take in the significance of his warning for they would have held the common belief that the coming of the kingdom would be glory all along the way even though it meant taking an unpopular political line. None could have foreseen a kingdom born out of Good Friday and Easter. But the warning of Jesus is there, and also the promise that some of those standing there would still be alive when the kingdom came with power after his victory at the first Easter.

Two Notes.

Prof. Caird draws attention to the fact that in none of the accounts of the feeding of crowds is there any mention that Jesus actually multiplied the loaves and fishes. The extraordinary feature was the large amount of food left over. My comment is that, although there is in the feedings a symbolism of the later Eucharist, it should be said that if

Jesus held such training sessions in Galilee, some catering would have been necessary.

Jesus did not attempt to patch up an old garment with a new piece of cloth, as he mentioned in another place, but called for a new start, a renewal of heart. This drastic reformation has been used throughout Christian history when church life has been at a low ebb. St Benedict, for example, five hundred years after his Lord, moulded unpromising material into an efficient community by insisting on a *conversatio morum* or a complete change of values.

Chapter 9: 28–36. The transfiguration.

In his book, *Jesus and the Victory of God*, Tom Wright confesses that he avoided until the last any mention of the transfiguration because it was not the kind of story one can make the basis of a historical reconstruction. Rather does its significance belong elsewhere. We should see it as part of a great mystical tradition which begins in the Old Testament with the prophetic experience of God and continues through Christian history until the present day. The researches of Evelyn Underhill and others in recent times show that intense devotions of saint and mystic have been accompanied by physical transformation and luminous glow. We are told this phenomenon happened when Jesus was praying and that the disciples were drawn into the experience.

Luke may see it as strengthening the inner circle of disciples as Jesus prepares them for the journey southward into more dangerous territory. Certainly it would be a further stage in the development of those who after the Lord's 'exodus' will continue the work of the kingdom.

The Greek word, *exodus* or departure is interesting for it takes us back to the great act of deliverance when Moses brought his people out of Egypt. Caird expresses the idea in lyrical fashion:

At Jerusalem Jesus was to accomplish the New Exodus, leading God's people from a greater bondage than that of Egypt into the promised land of the kingdom. Like Moses of old, he was now standing on the brink of a great sea, the ocean of iniquity through which he must pass and in which he must accomplish another baptism (12:50).[39]

The phrase 'sea of iniquity' is no flight of fancy if we have followed Jesus in his encounters so far with the devil.

Jesus is walking along a road which has been trodden by Moses and Elijah. 'Now God is about to lead him into a path never before trodden by human foot, a path which will lead him to Gethsemane and Calvary' (Caird).

All this is too much for Peter who wanted to capture the experience by building some sort of shrine as the Israelites had done in the wilderness to celebrate the glory of God. Peter did not realize that the old order of Moses and Elijah and even John the Baptist was passing away, and Jesus alone remained as God's Christ. 'This is my Son, my chosen; listen to him' (cp. Deut. 18:13). There was no need of three shrines because the divine glory was enshrined in Jesus.

Chapter 9:37–50. From the sublime to the ridiculous.

The transfiguration may be called a highlight of the Lord's earthly ministry. There is some debate about where it took place: some put it on the snowy hills of Hermon, which tower above Israel in the north; others think it a post-resurrection appearance. If it is placed within the training of disciples, Mount Tabor on the southern edge of the plain of Jezreel is the most likely site, and this is where today's pilgrims are taken. It is a brave person who actually climbs this sharp rise, and most go the easy way by taxi. Once at the top there is a heady view of the plain and countryside below, and it is easy to recapture the original episode.

From this other-worldly experience Jesus and the three disciples are quickly brought back to earth, for when they rejoin the others on the level, they find an almost farcical situation where a healing miracle had gone wrong, and everybody would have been gesticulating wildly. The father of the tormented boy brought him in desperation to Jesus who dealt with the evil spirit and cured him. As Raymond Brown notes, Luke uses the incident to show how the majesty of God is manifested.

Healing miracles, of course call not only for a right relationship between the healer and the patient but also for a reserve of spiritual power which the disciples obviously still have to develop.

Jesus now issues another warning about the suffering which he will have to undergo. This was contained in the transfiguration event – Jesus spoke with Moses and Elijah about his 'exodus'.

A further example of how much the disciples have to learn is shown in the way they quarrel about who should have the most important positions, no doubt in a kingdom which they still fix firmly on earth. They are given an example of humility through a small child, but are told that even an outsider who uses Jesus' name has a place. This is indeed being cut down to size!

Chapter 10:1–20. The mission of the Seventy-two.

It seems logical to include these verses before the next section of the Gospel which takes us further south, on the road to Jerusalem. If we have understood the Lord's method of organizing what Wright has called a campaign or revolutionary movement, we could see the feeding in the wilderness. (9:10–18) as a final training session. He now has trained people he can send into new territory where he is about to go. They can now proclaim a kingdom of God which is peace and not war. Jesus instructs them how they are to conduct themselves. They will not receive a friendly welcome everywhere, but towns which reject them will in the end regret it.

They return full of successes they have had, and Jesus sees this as a further defeat of the powers of evil. It has already been noted that the battle against Satan is never far from the mission of Jesus. This advance of the kingdom of God now calls forth a paean of thanks from Jesus to his Father. It has been hard work gathering disciples together, training them and showing them how great is their privilege in being part of so great an enterprise, but now suddenly initial difficulties are clearing away and he can advance into fresh territory. Now will come an even greater challenge further south in Jerusalem, but at least his followers have had some insight into the revelation which in time would uniquely belong to all Christians.

The Shape of the Gospels.

If we follow St John's Gospel, we learn that Our Lord's ministry lasted three years and that he was constantly on the move between north and south. During this time he was teaching either large crowds or individuals and small groups, and this meant that he left behind a considerable amount of material which had to be reduced to a manageable size. There was a limit to the amount which either a papyrus or codex could take.

The Gospel writers dealt with this material in different ways according to the needs of the community for which they were writing. Much has been written about the wording of each Gospel, what was included and what was excluded, and what the evangelists have in common, especially in the first three Gospels. Not so much has been written about their shapes or the different ways the material was arranged, and yet we can learn from these the purpose behind each Gospel.

First it should be noted that although Our Lord left behind a mass of teaching, there was a basic simple theme, and that was the kingdom of God and how his Jewish audiences should respond to its arrival. In his proclamation of this, Jesus would have repeated his teaching time and time again, adapting it no doubt to his different hearers. The Jew in the country districts of northern Galilee would need a different approach from the more sophisticated resident in Jerusalem and the south. The evangelists therefore had several versions of the same sayings and parables in front of them, and this would explain why they do not always agree. Yet the overall scenario is the same. Jesus is on the desperate mission of trying to turn his people back from the destruction to which they were heading through their desire for vengeance on those who had occupied their land.

The picture then which Jesus gave of his Father was not of one who favoured one nation at the expense of the rest of his creation. He was a loving father who welcomed all into his kingdom, Jew, Gentile, sinner and the outcast. We have an example today of the damage modern Judaism is causing by claiming an exclusive right to the land of Israel. There is a refusal to share their national life with non-Jews, and this can be traced back to Old Testament times. Think, for example, about what happened when the Jews returned from exile in Babylon (c. 500 BC) and began to rebuild their city and temple. Other people offered to help but were rudely rebuffed (Ezra 4). The Jews wanted no help from outsiders! What a chance of co-operation and peace was missed. This going-it-alone spirit continued to Our Lord's time, and was sending them on the road to destruction and exile. It was this spirit which Jesus sought to change, and suffered for it. This was the story which our Gospel writers set out to tell, in their different ways and within certain limitations. Luke, for example, was not a Jew and lived outside Israel, and therefore his geography is sometimes at fault. The Gospel he gives us is none the worse for this.

We are studying Luke's work and can follow the shape he used. At this stage, however, it might be helpful to learn how the other three evangelists handled the mass of material which has been described above. It will explain why they sometimes differ from Luke.

John.

The Gospel of John is in some ways the least complicated of the four. It appears to be a travelogue which takes us up and down Palestine showing how Jesus preached his kingdom in Galilee, Samaria and Jerusalem. We can therefore understand how, as he moves toward his crucifixion and death, he had friends and enemies in Jerusalem. We can also understand how he could weep over the city, for he had experienced the corrupt state of religion there. From John we learn that Our Lord had a three-year ministry, for three Passovers are mentioned. John writes from this side of the resurrection and so can see every word and deed of Jesus in the days of his earthly ministry as being shot through with risen glory. The life of the Lord can be entered in greater depth. No longer do we say of him, This is the Christ, but that we can see the Father in the Son – he is the Word (*Logos*).

If there is little mention of the kingdom, nevertheless there is much teaching about how members should behave within it – they should love each other. Perfect love is that seen within the Father–Son relationship. All are called upon to share in that love and pass it on to each other. Here John sums up similar teaching which can be found in the other gospels.

Mark.

Here we have a different shape. Mark's Gospel has a simple division into two parts, the ministry in Galilee, and in Jerusalem. It is short, and both starts and ends abruptly, making some scholars think that part of the original scroll has been lost. However, this theory is not necessary if we accept the idea that the gospel was written in Rome. Roman readers would not be interested in the childhood of Jesus, and did not need to be reminded of the risen appearances of the Lord, for they knew from life in the local community that he was alive (this is accepting the theory that the gospel ends at 16:8 and that the rest has been added later). In fact Mark's Gospel is just what we might expect from one who was writing for Romans who never used two words when one would do.

Matthew.

After his introduction of the infancy narrative the writer follows Mark in his account of the ministry, the preaching in Galilee, and the progress to Jerusalem ending with the Passion. He has one resurrection appearance. An interesting feature is the shape in which action is interspersed with five sections of teaching, which has made some scholars conclude that this is the New Law which restates the Old Law of Moses. This adds weight to the theory that the Gospel was written mainly for Jewish readers.

Luke.

We have learnt already that since Jesus was preaching the arrival of the kingdom of God he could be seen as being involved in serious political action, for a kingdom must of necessity have a king, it must have rules and also recognize who should be its citizens. So after setting his Gospel firmly within a Jewish scenario, Luke devotes chapters 4–9:50 to the organization of his kingdom in the country districts of northern Galilee. He proclaims the arrival of the kingdom of God, attracts followers including the Twelve, and trains them in isolated places until they are ready to be sent out to prepare the way for his further preaching. With this organization in place, Jesus moves south into more sophisticated areas where opposition leads to his death. Luke ends with accounts of resurrection appearances. Whereas we can place the first part of the Gospel in the north of Palestine, after chapter 10 Luke's geography is less reliable, understandable if he lived in another part of the Middle East. But by then he has made his point and shown how the mission, which had grown rapidly after Pentecost and reached Antioch in Syria and beyond, had started with Jesus. He composed a clear foundation for the events which he describes in the Acts of the Apostles.

Conclusion.

From this we may understand how the mass of material which the preaching of Jesus created was handled in different ways by four writers. A modern example can be found in the recent performance of Elgar's Third Symphony which the composer had left unfinished. Over a hundred sheets of manuscript contained sketches he had made for his work, and these were blended by a modern composer to produce a complete symphony. Here the task was not just joining pages together, nor of producing an entirely new work, but to let Elgar speak through the themes he had left.

This illustrates the evangelists at work on the material of the Lord's life which they had before them. Their Gospels would not be merely a joining-together of reminiscences and notes, but the presentation of the basic theme of the kingdom of God preached by Jesus, Son of God. In their different ways they tell the story of the ministry on earth of Jesus Christ, the Son of God, based on eye-witness accounts which were put together to support the preaching of the first apostles and their fellow-preachers. In the words of Professor Moule: 'The Synoptic Gospels present primarily the recognition that a vital element in evangelism is the plain story of what happened in the ministry of Jesus.' I would add that this would also apply to John. Moule continues by saying that John and Luke are more likely to have been read by the outsider, whereas Matthew and Mark may well represent instruction for Christians (op. cit. p.113).

TO THE SOUTH (CHAPTER 9:51—).

The Story so Far.

If we accept that Jesus was engaged in politics, albeit of a religious kind and in a thoroughly Jewish scene, we can see how, from chapter 4 onwards, he organized his campaign. I have already noted that anybody who talks about a kingdom must be concerned about who its citizens should be (*polis* is the Greek word for a city or state and *polites* the word for a citizen), how they should be governed and how they should behave. Jesus' main theme was the kingdom of God whose borders were wider and more friendly than that of the Jews of his time.

Jesus proclaimed the end of exile and the coming rule of God in his world. He received a mixed reception and organized a small following into a movement which met for instruction in quiet open spaces. His teaching found in the Sermon on the Plain called for co-operation everywhere rather than confrontation, for love and peace rather than hate and war. He showed his authority by wonderful works of healing in which the power of evil or Satan is met and defeated. He chose twelve men first as close disciples, and as his following grew he trained more 'activists' and sent them out to prepare a way before him in new territory. He warned them that the cost of following him could be great, and indicated that he had suffering and death to undergo.

It should be observed that the country district of Galilee was more suitable strategically for opening a campaign than the city and town life in the south round Jerusalem.

If we are worried about these political implications of the Gospel it should be realized that the setting up of a kingdom of God has been the concern of governments before and after the preaching of Jesus; we are still waiting for it to be implemented in our time, and so long as we delay bringing it in, the danger of world unrest and conflict is likely to destroy us all. Jesus knew that his people, the Jews, were on a collision course with a great military power and tried to show them another way. When towns like Chorazin, Bethsaida and Capernaum refused to listen to him he warned them of the dreadful consequences which would follow, not in the Last Judgement, but in the coming destruction of their land by the Romans.

We are now ready to follow Jesus as he takes his campaign to a different challenge in the south, where the opposition and questions would be more sophisticated than among country folk in Galilee. So far we have been able to follow the geography of Our Lord's ministry, but further south the picture is more complicated and we are often uncertain where the action is taking place. In John's Gospel we can follow Jesus as he moves round Palestine, but Luke's geography is not so good – understandable if we remember that he lived outside Israel and may not have visited it very often.

It seems right to start at 9:51–end and then move on to 10:25, when we are clearly in a different environment where farming illustrations give way to more sophisticated teaching, such as the Good Samaritan.

Chapter 9:51–6. Trouble on the way.

Samaria was a buffer zone between Galilee and Jerusalem, and Jews on the way south to carry out their duties in the temple often had to face aggressive opposition from the inhabitants, which could end in injury or even death. There was a long history of hostility between Jews and Samaritans which went back to the division of the kingdom, after Solomon's successful reign, into North and South, Israel and Judah. The schism became complete after the northern kingdom was defeated by Assyria *c.* BC 700 and many of its inhabitants deported. The king of Assyria brought foreigners into the land who intermarried with the Jews who were left behind, and became half-breeds in the eyes of Jews in the southern kingdom. Jerusalem in turn was destroyed in *c.* BC 600 and many were exiled to Babylon. When they returned from exile *c.* 500 the Samaritan community offered to help them rebuild the city and temple, but were rudely rebuffed (Ezra 4), and the chance of a united Holy Land was lost. This is another example of that Jewish exclusiveness which Jesus tried without success to reform. In time the Samaritans made their own place of worship on Mount Gerizim, near the modern Nablus, and this remains until today.

This diversion is necessary because Samaritans play a minor role in the Gospels, appearing in different guises.

Jews regarded them as lower even than foreigners. In John's Gospel Jesus makes friends in Samaria, and this connection seems to have lasted into the early Christian church.

The result of this unhappy history was that Jews from Galilee, passing through Samaria on the way to the temple, could be maltreated, and many preferred to travel south by a longer route.

Jesus and his disciples in Luke are unpleasantly received, and James and John wanted the same punishment meted out to the Samaritans as Elijah gave to soldiers sent to him by the king of Israel (2 Kings 1:9ff.). The disciples wanted nothing to hinder the progress of their master. Jesus rebuked them, and took a different route.

Chapter 9:57–end. The price of discipleship.

Jesus never leaves his followers in doubt about the possible cost of following him. No doubt rebel leaders of that time would have issued a similar warning. In 4 BC Pharisees who urged young hotheads to pull down the eagle from Herod's temple warned of the consequences, but this did not deter them. Jewish martyrs hoped that they would be vindicated by God.

Jesus goes further by calling possible recruits to his cause to sever their family ties, and in those days that was a more drastic action than we can realize today. As Wright notes, family and property were not for the ancient Jew what they are in our present western world. Both carried religious and cultural significance far beyond personal identity and security. Family duties too, like burying the dead, could only be neglected at the expense of cutting oneself off from the social past. It was just this which the teaching of Jesus required because Israel's concentration on nation and land was directing them to engage in a war they could not win. Jesus was resolutely opposed to such a holy war.

Chapter 10:25–37. The greatest law and the Good Samaritan.

We seem now to have reached the south, Jerusalem perhaps, a land of lawyers and rabbis. A lawyer asks a question, not because he wants to know the answer, but to test Jesus' competence to interpret the Scriptures. Jesus heads off an intellectual sparring match by turning the question back on the lawyer. He quotes the most famous of all Jewish prayers, the *Shema*, which was said every day. 'Hear, O Israel, the Lord your God is one God, and you shall love the Lord your God with all your heart, with all your soul, with all your strength and with all your mind' to which the words could be added 'and your neighbour as yourself'.

The lawyer is not satisfied and asks for elucidation of the word 'neighbour', to which Jesus replies with a brilliant miniature story which has enjoyed a universal appeal. Generally a good Samaritan is someone who helps another in distress, and this is exactly what the Samaritan in Jesus' story did. Yet the lesson was not meant to be merely one of moral encouragement but, like the rest of Our Lord's teaching, had to be seen against the background of the kingdom of God. It sought to answer the lawyer's question, Who is my neighbour? This was not asked frivolously, but because he knew his future salvation depended on keeping the *Shema* correctly and this involved knowing who his neighbour was. So he sought 'to justify himself' and this meant more than making an excuse for asking a silly or awkward question. The Greek word used here for justify is *dikaiein*, and this means 'to think right', and so to do the right thing, and the lawyer was anxious to know whom he should love, as the *Shema* ordered. The story becomes more complicated in the light of the Jewish situation of Jesus' day. Each character was governed by a particular life style: the priest could not perform his duties in the temple if he had been in contact with a dead body because the Law forbade it – the man in the ditch might have been dead. The Samaritan also would have been brought up to avoid contact with a Jew, and the stricken man might have resisted attempts by this outcast to treat him. In the end the Jew in the ditch discovered that this 'untouchable' was his neighbour, and that the other two were not, because the Law prevented them from being so.

So we have here more than a moral tale which has an added piquancy because the Jew and Samaritan were part of a long cultural feud. As Wright points out, the story dramatically redefines the covenant boundary of Israel, of the Torah or Law itself and even the temple cult.

> At stake throughout was the question: who would inherit the age to come? In other words, who would benefit when YHWH brought in the kingdom? The parable answered this question with sharp clarity. Outsiders were coming into the kingdom, and – at least by implication – insiders were being left out. More specifically, there was a way of being Israel which would be truly and radically faithful to the very centre of [the Law], as summed up in the *Shema*.[40]

At the end of the story Jesus asked the question, Who was neighbour to the one who fell among thieves? The answer was that the Jew in the ditch discovered that the Samaritan was his neighbour, and this broke down a barrier which had kept Jews apart from other peoples. So the Good Samaritan story may be seen as a part of the ongoing proclamation that the kingdom of God is for all, and not for Jews alone. The result was a challenge to the lawyer, not unlike Jesus' challenge to a rich young man who asked, 'What must I do to inherit the age to come?' The answer was: follow Jesus in finding a new and more radical version of the observance of the Law. Loving Israel's God meant loving him as creator of all, and discovering as one's neighbour those who might not belong to the chosen people. In this way, a person would be 'justified', would do the right thing and so would be vindicated

at the time of God's judgement. The lawyer was told to 'go
and do likewise'. We are not told if he had learnt his
lesson! All this was yet another example of Jesus' teaching
that many would come from east and west and sit down in
the kingdom of God, while the chosen people would be
left outside – not a comfortable message for his Jewish
hearers!

Chapter 10:38–42. Martha and Mary.

We have here a rare domestic interlude, matched only by
John 11:1ff. and 12:1ff. where the scene is Bethany. As we
have seen, Luke's geography is sketchy so this episode
might well have taken place in the same village near
Jerusalem.

Over the years the Christian Church has understood the
conversation between Mary, Martha and Jesus as showing
the contrast between the practical and the spiritual and the
priority of prayer over housework. But knowledge of
Palestinian village life in the first century alerts us to a
more subversive message. Mary is neglecting her duty of
serving tables to concentrate on the word of God and is
supported by Jesus. This may also be another example of
how Jesus saw his teaching about the kingdom of God as
having paramount importance.

Chapter 11:1–13. Lessons on prayer.

In response to a request from his disciples to give them a
lesson in prayer, Jesus taught them what has come to be
called the Lord's Prayer. This quickly became the Christian Church's prayer which is used on every possible occasion, public or private. If seen as part of Our Lord's
political campaign, however, it becomes more than a
bedside devotion, but rather a battle-cry. It must be seen
as an extraordinary, revolutionary and very Jewish
prayer. It echoes the desires of the Jewish people for God's
kingdom to arrive, but at the same time gives Our Lord's
reinterpretation of what that kingdom meant. The fact
that we have different versions of this prayer may be an

indication that Jesus taught not an exact form of words, understandable if they were repeated on many occasions, but a shape and pattern.

'Thy name be hallowed'. The prophet Ezekiel (chapter 36:22ff.) promised that God would bring his people back from exile to their own homeland in order that his name might be hallowed among the nations. The prayer asks that this may now be done.

'Thy kingdom come'. But in the way God wants, not the way the Jewish people want.

'Give us each day our daily bread'. Perhaps this should be seen alongside Jesus' words in Matthew 6:25ff. Also, a wandering preacher needs bread for one day only.

'Forgive us our sins'. Prayer for forgiveness and the accompanying requirement of forgiveness within the community is part of the whole emphasis on the inauguration of the new covenant (Wright).

'And do not bring us to the test (or trial)'. Jesus elsewhere warns about the coming disasters (21:20ff.), when the Romans will destroy their state. Jesus wants his people to be protected from the worst of this suffering.

'Save us from the evil one'. The real enemy is not Rome, but the evil one, who had to be guarded against continually.

We can see how the Lord's Prayer fits in perfectly with Jesus' preaching of the kingdom of his Father.

There follows some general teaching about praying confidently, based upon everyday practice. The story of the insistent friend reflects Palestinian custom where a whole family was crowded into a single-room house. An important Lucan addition is the promise of the Holy Spirit to those who ask.

The Battle Lines Drawn: Chapter 11:14–36.

This is a significant passage because it shows the widening gulf between Jesus and the Jewish religious authorities. The chief bone of contention was about who was Israel's enemy and how he should be fought. It should be remembered that since the exile to Babylon in 600 BC the Jews had been under constant occupation and longed for it to end. They drew hope from the Book of Daniel, which was rather like an Old Moore's Almanac, for it prophesied the future (Daniel 9:24–7; 2:35 and 44–5). After occupation by four great powers, Babylon, Persia, Greece and Rome, the Jews would come into their own again and God would act by ending the exile and bringing in his kingdom. Rome, therefore, was the last enemy to be defeated, and there was a simmering excitement about when and how this would happen. Jesus saw the real enemy to be defeated was Satan, or the power of evil, who had been the cause of the exile. Exorcisms, therefore, formed the central part of Jesus' work, which was not simply the end of suffering for a few sick people, but was the very essence of his mission. 'If I by the finger of God cast out devils, no doubt the kingdom of God has come upon you.'

This was not at all the programme which the religious authorities had in mind, and yet Jesus seemed to be successful, for devils were cast out. The people (Matthew 12:23) were even being converted to the idea that here was a new David who would fight their battles for them. There had to be another explanation, and so Jesus was accused of being in league with Satan. Jesus replies with logic, by saying that Satan's kingdom would have no future if it was divided.

So we can see from this that Jesus had drawn up his battle line against the power of evil, but that the Jewish authorities saw Rome as the enemy. Each demanded a different course of action. The Jews were preparing to take on their enemy with force; Jesus' method was preaching a gospel of love and reconciliation, shown in his treatment of those who suffered. In the eyes of his opponents he was undermining the military effort, and when he attacked the cherished symbols of Jewish religious life, the temple and the Law, they understood that he had to be silenced. But, of course, Jesus continued his work and preaching, and the gap widened until his opponents resorted to brute force.

Wright points out that an absolutely secure fact was that the early Church did not invent the charge that Jesus was possessed by the prince of demons. This is important negative evidence that Jesus did indeed perform exorcisms as a regular and controversial part of his ministry, and that this resulted in controversies like the present one. He continues by saying that this charge against Jesus was not just a bit of unpleasant religious propaganda. It was the only way that his opponents could avoid the clear implications of the ministry they were witnessing. When Jesus' commands to the devils were obeyed, there could be only one conclusion: Israel's god was at last becoming king. In the world of first-century Judaism, someone who did such things was either from the true god or from the enemy.

Jesus knew that he was winning his battle. Had he not faced Satan in the temptations in the wilderness and defeated him? When some of his followers went on a preaching mission and carried on his work even further he could say: 'I saw the satan fall like lightning from heaven (Luke 10:18).

Some may see in these verses an echo of the confrontation Jesus had with the Pharisees in the Temple and reported in John 8.

Matthew 12:31–2 adds a warning about sin against the Holy Spirit. To call good bad and vice versa is a hopeless condition. *Corruptio optimi, pessima* – corruption of the best is the worst state of perversion. There was no place in Our Lord's following for such people nor for those who remain neutral (Luke 11:23).

Chapter 11:24–6. The seven other demons.

Jesus is not speaking here about the temporary nature of exorcisms, because this might show that he had not won a decisive victory. This could well be a parable about Israel and the different movements which had been intended to give a fresh start. The example of the Maccabaeans comes to mind. They had swept the Greeks out of the land and put their house in order, only for the Jews eventually to return to the bad old days. Or was this a reference to the rebuilding of the temple? What good would it be to have a magnificent new building if the whole system was not reformed? An example from modern life can further illustrate the point. We are talking about colonizing the Moon, and some see it as a chance of getting away from the many troubles we have on earth. But if the colonizers do not change their life style completely we shall only be transferring our mistakes to another planet.

Some words of St Augustine come to mind. He says God wants to fill us with honey but if we are already filled with vinegar, he cannot do it. First the vinegar has to be emptied out, and the jar cleansed, then the honey may be poured in. This would explain what Jesus was saying. It is no good casting out devils and leaving a vacuum: something good has to be substituted, and this meant his teaching about the kingdom of God. His words to the woman who called him blessed emphasize this – (11:27–8) rather, blessed are those who hear the word of God and keep it.

Chapter 11:29–32. The call for another sign.

Jesus had already given ample evidence that the kingdom of God was at work and had called people to change their lives accordingly, just as Jonah had called the people of Nineveh to repentance, and they had responded. So Jesus was calling for a complete change of lives, but was not being heard. His words of wisdom were falling on deaf ears. In vain would the Jews remember Jonah and the Queen of the South when judgement day came and the Romans were destroying their city and state.

Jesus was not doing remarkable things for his own good: to give way to the people's request would give the wrong message.

Chapter 11:33–6. Light for the world.

The Jews were meant to be a light to the world according to the prophet Isaiah, but if they are blind themselves, how can they be faithful to their mission? If the light in them was darkness they were in a desperate situation.

Chapter 11:37ff. The trouble with law.

In this incident in the Pharisee's house we have a practical example of how obsession with the Law can divert people from the real issues of life. Caird doubts whether Jesus really laid into his critics in such forthright terms but it would be in line with the uncompromising approach else-where.

A Diversion on Law.

Throughout the gospel we find Jesus in confrontation with the scribes and Pharisees over the keeping of the Law, or at least the misuse of it. Living by a system of laws has always been a feature of religion in general. It began long before Moses gave the commandments to the Jews. A Babylonian code of laws put together about 1700 BC by King Hammurabi shows an early attempt to regulate daily life. Law, however, has a habit of multiplying itself and herein is one of its dangers. It starts with a few regulations and then gradually increases until man is overwhelmed and chained by them. The ten commandments in Exodus soon became a massive legal system which infiltrated every field of life, putting man under a kind of tyranny. By the time of Jesus there were 613 commandments to be kept by the Jews. Through the keeping of the Law a man became 'right-eous' before God and so could expect a favourable verdict when judgement came. There developed a division between those who could study the intricacies of the Law and those whose way of life made this impossible. 'This people who know not the Law are cursed' (John 7:49). Some Jews made the study of the Law a lifelong way of life and could say with the Psalmist, 'Lord, how I love your law, my study is in it.' It was said that immersing oneself in the Law was to be in the presence of God.

Some of its regulations set the Jews apart when they had to live among foreigners: for example, the keeping of the sabbath and food laws. This was useful during the exile in Babylon when they could easily have merged with their captors. They had lost their land and their temple but at least they had a distinctive way of life. They needed this at that time to keep their identity as a special people but, as we shall see, this became an obstacle to their mission when they returned to Israel.

It is clear that law is essential in everyday social life but why is it out of place as a main driving force in religion? First, law sets a limit to the amount a person has to do for God, leaving loopholes for man to get on with his own private sector. Religion here becomes a limited thing instead of a complete dedication to the service of God. Next, the mere keeping of laws induces a certain self-satisfaction, or pride, complacency. The example of the scribes and Pharisees in the Bible is an example of this. The slavish keeping of the rules leads to the idea that one has a claim on God: that I actually deserve to be rewarded.

We should not forget that law evasion flourishes when the rules are too strict. This leads to casuistry by which the load may be eased. So a man's religion may become less committed and in the end not much more than obeying a few outward rites and requirements. Finally, religion governed by law may bring the idea of fear: if I do not keep the rules I shall be punished.

It can be recognized that these perversions of law could not fit in with Our Lord's teaching and that he had an obligation to condemn them. But there was another reason why the Law formed an obstacle to his teaching. Together with the temple and the land, the Law threw a bulwark or fence round the chosen people and kept them separate from all other peoples. The Son of God had come to offer salvation to all his Father's creation, foreigners, outcasts and sinners, and therefore any restrictions on his mission could not be acceptable and must be challenged. It is easy to understand why the religious authorities viewed his attacks on their exclusiveness with anger and hostility.

If Our Lord's attack on the religious authorities seems harsh (11:42–54), it was made at a time of great national emergency. Reliance on the Law was driving the Jews to a collision course with the mighty power of Rome, and if it seemed an unequal conflict nevertheless they believed the rightness of their cause would ensure that God would intervene on their side. We are not short of modern examples of the same motivation. There are militant groups in the Middle East who are fanatically convinced of the rightness of their cause and oblivious to any arguments to the contrary, not least because they believe, like Lebanese Muslims etc. in a close connection between martyrdom and eternal bliss.

In modern times, also, we have seen desperate attempts to avert wars threatening to lead to a third world war which could destroy most of the human race. The situation in first-century Palestine was a microcosm of what we fear today, and we can understand Jesus' desperate campaign to create a new spirit in his people which would save them from total disaster. This theme of judgement upon the present generation can be seen in chapters 11 to 19 of Luke's Gospel as well as in the other Synoptics.

In Luke 11:42ff., therefore, we find Jesus attacking the Pharisees on different counts: they are so concerned with small details, such as ritual purity, that they cannot see the dreadful disease which is growing within Israel; they are bad examples to those whom they are supposed to lead: such a way of life resisted the attempts of prophets over the years to reform their people. In vain would be the coming kingdom of God if it were to be filled with such citizens.

The Life Style of Disciples: Chapter 12—.

Our Lord therefore drew up his own battle line of followers who would be led not by a love of law but rather by a law of love which enclosed all his Father's creation. The teaching of the Law or Torah would be replaced by himself who was showing how this law of love worked out in everyday life. He drew men and women to himself and gave them his own way of life. This was the way of light which would not be covered up or hidden (12:1–3). They were a 'little flock' at present and lived in great danger. Their real enemy would not be hostile Jewish authorities or the Romans, but rather the evil one who had power to cast into hell or gehenna (12:4–5). They must not be frightened, because they were in the care of God and therefore need not be afraid of being in Jesus' battle line.

If necessary they must give up all, because the cause was too great for half measures. Rights to property therefore were irrelevant (12:13–22) and Jesus was not prepared to make them his province. Rather did they belong to Caesar, and anyway were an unreliable source of security.

In view of all this Jesus spelt out a way of life which put food, clothes and possessions in perspective. The important object of life was the kingdom which God would give to those who made it their real treasure.

A disciple's life style therefore would be like that of servants who wait for their master's return from a wedding party. He in turn would serve them. However, nobody knew when this would happen, and so all had to be waiting. There are a number of parables on this theme of a master or king returning and expecting to find servants ready to greet him and there has been much speculation about what Jesus meant. Was this a reference of the early Church to the expected return of Jesus, was it the appearance of the Son of Man, the coming climax to Jesus' ministry or a judgement on the nation of Israel? Both Wright and Caird dismiss the idea that Jesus was speaking about his second coming. As Caird writes, 'it is hardly credible that he should have required his disciples during his lifetime to be on guard night and day for an emergency which, to say the least of it, could not happen for some time after his death.'

Some scholars have supposed that the return of a king or master refers to the return of Jesus himself, and this has become accepted by modern readers. But other scholars have agreed with Caird that Jesus did not speak of his own return, and that such stories are the work of the early Church through the evangelists and their sources.

Wright has another solution and suggests we put ourselves into the mind of a first-century Jew who lived in the hope of God's return to Sion and the end of the Babylonian exile. As at the first exodus he would come and dwell among his people and speak to them (Exodus 19:9 etc.) so that Jews no doubt would have been fed on the comforting words of the prophets, especially Isaiah. Readings which Christians use today in the season of Advent and Christmas to proclaim the coming of their Saviour were applied by the Jews of Jesus' day to the return of their God to Sion. Ezekiel had seen the glory of God depart from the city at the time of the exile (11:12ff.) and since then Jews had looked for his return. They could receive encouragement from Isaiah and other prophets such as Zechariah and Malachi:

> Get you up to a high mountain,
> O Sion, herald of good tidings;
> lift up your voice with strength,
> O Jerusalem, herald of good tidings,
> lift it up, do not fear;
> say to the cities of Judah,
> 'Here is your God!'
> See the Lord YHWH comes with might,
> and his arm rules for him;
> his reward is with him,
> and his recompense before him (Isaiah 40:9–11).

How beautiful upon the mountains
are the feet of the messenger who announces peace,
who brings good news, who announces salvation,
who says to Zion, 'Your God reigns'.
Listen! Your sentinels lift up their voices,
together they sing for joy;
for in plain sight they see
the return of YHWH to Sion (Isaiah 52:7–10).

Ezekiel (43:1–7) could be even more definite for he saw the glory of the Lord entering the temple by the gate facing east: 'the spirit lifted me up, and brought me into the inner court; and the glory of YHWH filled the temple'.

But it might not be all joy, as Malachi warns; 'But who can endure the day of his coming, and who can stand when he appears?' (Mal.3:2). Even before the exile, Amos also could warn those in Judah who longed for the day of the Lord that it could be 'darkness and not light'.

There was therefore much evidence that most Jews of Jesus' day were hoping for God to return to dwell among them again. This hope was linked with a return from exile and the defeat of evil. In the writings of the time, not least in the Qumran scrolls, there was also the idea expressed that God might act through an agent. Do we get here a hint of the meaning of the title 'Son of Man' as mentioned in Daniel 7?

This is not the place to develop this idea, which has been widely and differently debated. Enough has been written to suggest that Jesus in his parables about a king or master going away and returning was referring to an expected return of God to his people. Far from it being a joyous occasion, it could be one of gloom and judgement as prophets had warned. It was therefore the time for the disciples of Jesus to strengthen their resolve, to get their priorities right and not be afraid of persecution. Their hearts might fail them when they saw the opposition drawn up against them, but the real enemy was Satan or the evil one. Jesus gives encouragement to his 'little flock':

'Have no fear: your Father has chosen to give you the kingdom.' They must therefore provide for themselves purses which do not wear out, and a never-failing treasure in heaven (Luke 12:33).

Jesus meanwhile continues his way into Jerusalem, knowing that he has a baptism of suffering to undergo, but wishing to precipitate the coming of the kingdom (12:49–50), a coming that will mean division where one might have expected unity (12:51–2). This division his followers might well have experienced already when they threw in their lot with Jesus. As we have seen earlier, a minority group could well have broken up families and villages. There was a pressing need to understand the sign of the times, just as people predicted the weather; to settle with the accuser while there was still time, lest one be convicted, sentenced and imprisoned (12:54–9) and to repent in order to escape the dreadful judgement whose main features will be slaughter in the temple precincts, and the crash of falling buildings (13:1–5). Jesus now gives another parable whose meaning could not be mistaken. God was now giving his people a last chance to change their ways before he came with judgement (13:6–9).

Jesus' whole progress to Jerusalem could be seen as a preparation for the eventual return of God to his holy mountain of Sion. Jesus was like a master coming back to his servants, or the owner to his vineyard. Those who did not read the signs of the times, who did not repent or follow his way of peace would be courting a disaster for which Pilate's small-scale act of brutality would be merely a foretaste (Wright).

By stating that he had a baptism to be baptized with, Jesus showed that this would happen in Jerusalem, who killed the prophets and stoned messengers sent to it (13:34). He had done everything possible to avert disaster, but to no avail, and he could only weep over the city.

Back on the Campaign Trail: (Chapter 14—).

Jesus continued to go through towns and villages, speaking with an authority which made people sit up and take notice, even if they did not join him. It was an authority which came from the originality of his teaching. As Wright notes, he was not simply reshuffling the cards already dealt, words of God spoken in former times. He was announcing a message from God. He was a herald like a Greek *kerux* (we get our word kerygma from him) whose duty it was to announce news of great importance in an ancient world where modern means of communication were absent. So a herald might go into a market place or *agora* and proclaim that war had broken out, an enemy was invading or peace had been declared. Citizens could then take appropriate action just as, in the last war, blackouts, rationing and air-raid shelters followed the radio announcement that we were at war with Germany. Jesus was such a herald who had an urgent message to proclaim which could not wait, could not become the stuff of academic debate. To use Wright's illustration, Jesus was 'like somebody driving through a town with a loudhailer' or 'like a man with a red flag heading off an imminent railway disaster.'

Wright also suggests that Jesus was 'like a politician on the campaign trail [rather] than a schoolmaster; more like a composer/conductor than a violin teacher; more like a subversive playwright than an actor'. It was action fraught with danger for he was trying to break down a narrow, exclusive way of life which had existed for much of Israel's history and had been the cause of its disasters. Since this exclusiveness was centred round Land, Temple and Law, cherished symbols of Jewish faith and practice, Jesus provoked first alarm, then violent hostility, when he attacked them.

This political role comes as a contrast to the modern idea of Jesus as the teacher of timeless truths and a moral leader, yet he was proclaiming a kingdom which demanded a complete change of heart from its citizens, and this has always been essential for the continuation of the victorious kingdom of God beyond Easter and Pentecost. The Benedictine rule that 'the brethren should serve each other' came straight from the Sermon on the Mount and is essential in any community.

For his mission Jesus used several techniques. He taught not only in parables but with other stories, cryptic sayings which could be remembered and repeated (about salt, light and leaven, 'the first shall be last', etc.) and wonderful works – the catch of fish, the stilling of a storm and the feeding of a large number of people in a desert place. Most vividly he showed by his exorcisms that he was able to defeat that scourge of the Jewish people, Satan or the power of evil.

Parables.

This is the method of teaching with which Jesus is most associated and many scholars have tried their hand at helping us to understand it; C.H. Dodd and Jeremias are examples. There was nothing original in this speaking in parables, for we can find models in the Old Testament: for example, Isaiah's parable of the vineyard, Ezekiel's sheep and shepherds, and not least the striking parable of the valley of bones. The very relationship of God with his people Israel could only be understood by means of stories. Jesus continued this method, and parables of the Good Samaritan, the Prodigal Son, the Sheep and Goats, are well-known today. There is, however, a danger of oversimplification, as we have already seen in notes on the Good Samaritan: here it was more than just the duty of helping others, but rather changing one's attitude to somebody who was an outcast.

The original use of parable by Jesus was more profound than just teaching some feature of individual spiritual life. It showed how God was coming into his kingdom and how his people should respond. In a nation resistant to Jesus' teaching a parable could be a time bomb thrown into a community where God's purpose had been entirely forgotten. An anecdote might appear innocent enough until its full implication was realized. Jesus warned about this when he said, 'He that has ears to hear, let him hear'. Parables do not merely give people something to think about; they invite them into the new world which is being created. Woe to him who refuses to enter!

Jews knew their history very well because they heard it read regularly in the synagogue. Jesus entered into this story but gave it a different twist. To sum up in Wright's words:

> the parables made sense only within the whole context of Jesus' career. They echoed, reflected, interpreted and indeed defended the main thrusts of Jesus' work, and themselves set up other echoes in turn. The parables functioned the way all (good) stories function, by inviting hearers into the world of the story. They were designed to break open worldviews and to create new ones, encouraging listeners to identify themselves in terms of the narrative. To see the point of the parable was to make a judgement on oneself.[41]

With these themes in mind we are able to return to the gospel narrative and follow Jesus in his deeds and words until those in authority could take no more and determined to destroy him. So far Jesus had escaped because of his itinerant ministry, but in Jerusalem there was no hiding place, and he knew that it could only be a matter of time before the powers of darkness closed in on him. So he did not heed the Pharisees' warning that Herod wanted to kill him (13:31–3) because 'it was unthinkable for a prophet to meet his death anywhere but in Jerusalem.' Jerusalem is about to face the equivalent of a devastating farmyard fire seen from the point of view of the livestock (the chicken). Jesus longed to do what mother hens do in such circumstances, but the chicks are refusing to come under his wings. As a result the temple is abandoned by

God and left to its fate, just as Ezekiel (chap. 10) had prophesied. If only Jews had greeted him as a pilgrim with the words 'Blessed is he who comes in the name of the Lord'! But they did not.

Chapter 14:1–5. Healing on the Sabbath.

The Pharisees will have been puzzled by Jesus' identity. In many ways he seemed to belong to their number, and then he would break ranks. So they watched for any differences, and here was one. The Sabbath as a day of rest was an important symbol of their exclusiveness, but it also foreshadowed the final great day of their liberation from slavery to foreigners. Jesus explains his action by indicating how they got round the Law when it suited them. A human being no matter how lowly was important in the eyes of God – 'even a sparrow does not fall to the ground unknown to God – you are more important than many sparrows'.

Chapter 14:7–24. Some lessons from meals.

The custom of giving banquets has long been both a form of entertainment and also a means of displaying social standing. It continues in this country still at state banquets, when great care is taken to seat people in their right place. Not everybody has seen such occasions in the same way. The Younger Pliny (first century AD) said he invited people for a meal and not for social distinction. A well-known host in America was asked how he seated his distinguished guests, and said, 'I take the line that those who matter don't mind, and those who mind don't matter'.

No doubt Our Lord would have approved of this principle when he saw the scramble for the best places at a wedding feast. The Pharisees and other religious authorities would have expected the best places because they were strict keepers of the Law. We have already seen the dangers of this way of life. It can make such people think that they have a claim on God because they keep his Law strictly. It can also give a sense of superiority over those who are not such experts. Jesus will have none of this and invokes the virtue of humility, as well as making a practical point of avoiding later embarrassment.

There is a further lesson behind these feasting stories. It was believed by the Jews that when the kingdom of God finally came there would be a great banquet to which his chosen ones would be invited. It was assumed that those who had kept the Law properly would qualify for this honour. Jesus overturns such expectation and teaches that the most unlikely people would find their way into the kingdom first. Here he extends the lesson he has shown in his daily dealing with the outcast, the poor and the sick. It is the Good Samaritan parable taken a step further.

The feast illustration is emphasized by the next parable (14:16–24) where many invitations are sent out but excuses are made. 'I cannot come because . . .'. Here we can recognize those who were not accepting the way of life Jesus was teaching. They would be shut out of the kingdom, whereas the underprivileged would be let in. It was not the kind of lesson which the Jewish leaders were likely to welcome.

Chapter 14:14. An interesting verse.

Caird has this comment. 'The loving service of the helpless and needy, which Jesus himself exemplified, is the very life of the kingdom of God, and those who learn on earth to enjoy such a life will enjoy the perfection of it in heaven.' What we might call an eschatological thought, as Raymond Brown notes.

Chapter 14:25ff. Danger Ahead!

There would have been Galileans travelling toward Jerusalem and some might think it was a triumphal procession. Jesus warned them that discipleship involved harsh decisions which could end in suffering. We have already seen how following Jesus could divide a village, even a family, but he wants nobody to be 'swept into the kingdom on a flood-tide of emotion', as Caird puts it. Careful consideration of the cost must be made. Wright notes that other rebel leaders might have said the same thing to their followers. 'The Pharisees who urged the young hotheads to pull down the eagle from Herod's temple [in 4 BC] issued a similar call'. Yet Jewish martyrs no doubt would have taken the risk, knowing that they would be vindicated by God.

What we can say is that 'to risk all in following Jesus places him and his followers firmly on the map of first-century socially and politically subversive movements' (Wright).

Sinners, the Lost Sheep and Coin, and the Prodigal Son: Chapter 15.

Chapter 15:1–3. Who are the sinners?

For most of Christian history there has been a clear understanding about who are saints and who are sinners. Saints are those who do the will of God as interpreted by the Church, and sinners are those who do not. In Our Lord's time the position was more complicated and not always judged by moral standards. For day-to-day sins a Jew could go to the temple and make a sin-offering, perhaps using a penitential psalm, such as 51. In the verses above, 'sinners' seems to denote something else, those outside the Jewish Law. The most extreme examples were foreigners, heathen or pagans: for these there was little hope of salvation. The next were 'people of the land', those descended from the Jews who were left behind at the exile in 600 BC and who had intermarried with foreigners, half-breeds, perhaps. The Samaritans were in this category, and they had compounded their 'sin' by setting up a rival place of worship on Mount Gerizim. Next there were Jews who did not know the Law, but they were reckoned to be second-class citizens rather than sinners. Then there were Jews whose occupations barred them from normal Jewish society. They were a mixed bunch: customs officers, tax collectors, shepherds, donkey drivers, pedlars and tanners (Jeremias). Finally, there were those who notoriously lived an immoral life; swindlers, adulterers and prostitutes. It is likely that Jesus was accused of eating with the last two groups.

Chapter 15:4–10. The Lost Sheep and Coin.

Jeremias notes that no shepherd in his right mind would leave the main flock and go after one animal which had wandered off.[42] When a sheep is lost it lies down dejectedly, and neither stands up or runs. So the shepherd has to carry it round his neck. Perhaps this parable underlines the almost insane love which God has for a lost sinner. As we shall see, this is matched by the behaviour of the father of the prodigal son. Generally, these two parables sound a note of desperation that a sinner should be saved. Wright notes that:

> Jesus frequently likens his work to that of a shepherd . . . He commands the disciples to go to the lost sheep of the house of Israel, and explains his own work in terms of the same task. The disciples themselves are to be like sheep or lambs; they are the 'little flock' to whom the Father will give the kingdom.

Here he uses a parable to explain his own ministry of welcome to outcasts. He called up the image of the shepherd of his people, a royal symbol in the Old Testament. Here God is the shepherd of his people, taking over from the false shepherds who had been feeding themselves instead of the sheep (see Isaiah, Jeremiah and Ezekiel). Now the sign that the exile was over and the kingdom of God had come could be seen in the urgency with which Jesus went to the lost sheep of the house of Israel. This was indeed prophecy come true!

Chapter 15:11–end. The Prodigal Son.

Like the Good Samaritan parable this has been loosely interpreted, as the person who has seriously sinned and has repented of his ways, perhaps returning to the ministrations of the Church. The sinner seeks the confessional and confesses his sins, while respectable church people are shocked that he can be accepted back into normal church life.

However, Wright suggests that the Prodigal Son parable should be seen as part of Jesus' teaching that the long exile had ended, the kingdom of God had come and forgiveness was now offered to all, outcasts included. The elder son becomes the self-righteous Jew who has faithfully kept the Law and who was certain that he would be given a place in the coming kingdom of God, while sinners had no chance. Wright says that most commentaries seem to miss the point of this parable. 'Here is a son who goes off in disgrace into a far country and then comes back, only to find the welcome challenged by another son who has [remained at home].' Here, believes Wright, is the story of Israel as seen in books of the Old Testament. My mind turns to the last chapter of 2 Chronicles where the last days of the Jews are recorded before going into exile to Babylon:

All the chiefs of Judah and the priests and the people became more and more unfaithful, following all the abominable practices of the other nations: and they defiled the house of the Lord which he had hallowed in Jerusalem.

The Lord God of their fathers had warned time and time again through his messengers, for he took pity on his people and on his dwelling place: but they never ceased to deride his messengers, scorn his words and scoff at his prophets until the anger of the Lord burst out against his people and could not be appeased. He brought against them the king of the Chaldaeans, who put their young men to the sword in the sanctuary and spared neither young man nor maiden, neither the old nor the weak; God gave them all into his power.

So Israel goes off to a pagan country, becomes a slave, and then is brought back to her own land. Exile and restoration is the main theme. But although, after the fall of Babylon, the Jews had returned, the great prophecies of restoration had not yet happened, and in Jesus' day most believed the exile was still continuing. Wright asks the question, 'What was Israel to do? Why, to repent of the sin which had driven her into exile, and to return to YHWH with all her heart. Who would stand in her way, to prevent her return?' The books of Ezra and Nehemiah tell us that the mixed population, including the Samaritans, who had remained in the land and had everything to lose by such a return, tried to prevent the rebuilding of Jerusalem and the temple. But the returned exiles succeeded, yet looked forward to a complete restoration in the future when YHWH would finally become king and do for Israel, in a renewal of his covenant, what the prophets had foretold.

Wright sums up the situation:

Exile and restoration; this is the central drama that Israel believed herself to be acting out. And the story of the prodigal says, quite simply: this hope [of Israel] is now being fulfilled ... Israel went into exile because of her own folly and disobedience, and is now returning because of the fantastically generous, indeed prodigal, love of her god.

'Prodigal' means generously lavish – and this can describe the behaviour of the father rather than the son.[43]

One needs to understand the relationship of a son to his father in Jesus' time. For a younger son to ask for his share of the inheritance was almost unthinkable. It was like saying 'I wish you were dead'. But the father agrees: the son goes off, and ends in poverty and degradation, but returns, prepared to be taken back as a slave. But the father runs to greet him and not only takes him back as a son but celebrates the occasion. The only sour note belongs to the elder son, who complains about the mad love of his father. The latter tries to reason with him, and here the story ends. If we identify the elder son with those who opposed Jesus' teaching, the door is left open for them to see sense in the future.

So the parable of the prodigal son becomes on reflection the story of a prodigal father. Most commentators compare the actions of the father with the loving-kindness of God to the sinner, but if we accept the political background to Luke's Gospel then we have to set this parable within a wider scenario. Wright goes even further by saying that the exile itself was seen as an illustration of God's dealing with his people.

> Israel could be allowed to sin, to follow pagan idolatry, even to end up feeding the pigs for a pagan master, but she could not fall out of the covenant purposes of her god. She could say to her god, 'I wish you were dead,' but her god would not respond in kind. When Israel comes to her senses there is an astonishingly [generous] welcome waiting for her.

Wright notes that in the celebratory meal for the returned son, Jesus is explaining why he eats with sinners. This is exactly how his Father acts in welcoming sinners so long as they accept the welcome of Jesus.

As was noted earlier, parables seek not only to teach but to bring hearers into the action. So this story creates a new world, and objectors are warned of the consequences of their action. They are like Pharaoh at the time of the Exodus from Egypt, or like the Samaritans who opposed the returning exiles from Babylon. The open-ended conclusion of the parable shows there is still time for objectors to change their minds, and confronts all with a choice, warning and an invitation.

Parables are never simple stories but leave hearers with

much to think about. So this parable of the returning son not only teaches the forgiveness of a penitent sinner but illustrates what Jesus was trying to do throughout his ministry. It is, therefore, a key to the whole of Luke's Gospel.

Here I must acknowledge my debt to Tom Wright for opening my eyes to the full implications of this well-known parable. His full account can be found in chapter 4 of his book *Jesus and the Victory of God*.

Problem passages: Chapter 16.

This chapter contains teachings which have posed problems for commentators. In the case of the Unjust Steward perhaps Luke himself had difficulty in understanding its implications, and this makes it very unlikely that a later generation invented it. Then there are sayings about money and marriage, ending with another problem parable or story, the rich man and Lazarus. As we shall see, it is safe to assume that Our Lord was putting all in the context of the kingdom of God and the coming crisis.

The Unjust Steward.

We have to ask several questions. Was the steward unjust because in the first place he had mismanaged his master's estate, or because he made a fraudulent deal with his clients? Who was the master? It could scarcely have been the owner of the property, because he was the loser in the transaction. Was it Jesus or God? Wright says that when master or lord is mentioned, it mostly refers to Israel's God. In any case the steward is commended because in commercial life he is acting with greater enterprise than people show in religious matters. Perhaps Luke is using this typical Jewish situation to teach the early Christian community the right use of wealth. It was, after all, known for the way members shared their goods.

But what did Jesus mean by this story, which may have been taken from an actual incident which had been reported to him? Caird says it must have been a parable of crisis, a warning from Jesus to his contemporaries to take resolute and immediate action in the face of impending disaster. He continues: 'When the crisis of the crucifixion had passed and the story came to be used for homiletic purposes in the early Church, it was taken to be a lesson on the right and wrong use of money and attracted to itself a series of unrelated sayings'. Wright also thinks that it is a parable of crisis. 'The steward is about to be put out of his stewardship, and if he knew his business he would be looking around for all the friends he could get while there is time.'[44]

Jeremias sums up the crisis factor:

As in the parable of the Burglar (Luke 12:39), Jesus is probably dealing with an actual case which had been indignantly reported to him. He deliberately chose it as an example, as he could be sure that it would secure the redoubled attention of any hearers who did not know of the incident. They would expect him to end the story with an expression of strong disapproval but instead of that, to their complete surprise, he praises the swindler. 'Are you indignant? Apply the lesson to yourselves. You are in the same position as that steward who saw disaster, his life in ruins: but the crisis that threatens you – in fact you are already involved in it – is comparably more terrible ... For you, too, the challenge of the hour demands prudence; everything is at stake.'

Jeremias continues: 'In face of this challenge of the hour, evasion is impossible. That is [also] the message of the parable of the Rich Man and Lazarus.'[45] We shall come to that when we have dealt with the next difficult sentences.

Chapter 16:10–15. Money and its problems.

Caird notes that all the opportunities of this world are tests of character, and by his behaviour in small matters a man shows if he is fit for larger responsibilities. It is 'unrighteous Mammon' because where there is money, there is menace – a lesson we have come to learn in modern times! Money 'is the great rival of God for the devotion and service of men' (Caird).

Chapter 16:14–18. More difficult passages.

Wright suggests we should interpret cryptic sayings of Jesus in the light of his teaching about the kingdom of God.

Chapter 16:14–15. Attack on the Pharisees.

There is no reason to suppose that they were worse than the other religious parties; the priestly party certainly enjoyed the good things of this life. Jesus is referring to the way they treated Israel's God as a faceless bureaucrat to be bribed or prayed into giving them what they wanted. Above all they wanted the restoration of land, property and ancestral rights, and this was serving Mammon instead of seeking the true kingdom. Caird notes that the Pharisees tended to treat prosperity as a reward for godliness (a belief found in the Old Testament), and this was detestable or an abomination (*bdelugma* in Greek) to God. 'Abomination' always denotes idolatry in the Bible. Almsgiving, prayer and fasting were three features of religious observance and regarded by some Pharisees as an equivalent to offering sacrifices in the temple.

Chapter 16:16.

The first part of this saying provides no problem. The prophets, even John the Baptist, belong to past history. The new age of the kingdom has arrived.

The words 'forcing their way in' are difficult. It can mean (Caird) that men of determination and energy are forcing their way in to it. Wright thinks it could be read as an ironic, and laconic, comment on the presence of the inbreaking kingdom: 'yes, and the men of violence are trying either to hijack the movement for their own ends, or, perhaps, to use violence against it.'

Chapter 16:17.

This could mean that although Our Lord made the Law obsolete, its moral principles remain. Caird says this is forcing the text too much and that it might be an ironic attack on the pedantic conservatism of the scribes: it is easier for heaven and earth to pass away than for the scribes to surrender even one iota of the Law.

Chapter 16:18.

This saying on divorce and marriage has caused debate, especially since Matthew gives a different version – 'except for fornication (*porneia*)'. But if we interpret the words within the rest of Our Lord's teaching, we might understand it to mean that in the future ideal life style of the kingdom of God there would be no cause for disagreement leading to divorce.

Chapter 16:19–31. The rich man and Lazarus.

There is agreement that Jesus is using a well-known folk story. Some scholars think it was told simply for the final twist: 'neither will they believe though one rose from the dead', a reference to the Lord's resurrection. Jeremias, however, thinks that Jesus tells the parable to warn people about the impending fate. Lazarus is merely a secondary figure introduced for contrast. He suggests that it should be called the parable of the Six Brothers. They live in selfish luxury like their dead brother. There would be no point in performing a miracle. He who will not submit to the word of God will not be converted by a miracle.'

Wright says that this is not a description of the afterlife, warning people of their ultimate destination. The welcome of Lazarus by Abraham echoes the welcome of the prodigal son by the father. Just as the poor and outcast would be welcomed into Abraham's bosom, so Jesus was welcoming these unlikely people into his kingdom. The parable describes what was happening to rich and poor at the present time when Jesus was proclaiming the true kingdom of God – a new age was dawning.

Some Rules on Behaviour: Chapter 17:1–11.

Scholars who attribute the composition of the gospels to a later date have placed these sayings within a developing Christian community, but, as we have seen earlier, there is no reason for supposing that Jesus was not giving advice on conduct to groups of his followers who could be found in the different towns and villages of Palestine. It was important that they should be above reproach in their dealings with each other.

There is a doubt whether 'little ones' refers to new disciples or children but it is probably right to assume the latter. Jesus has elsewhere (Mark 9:41) shown his concern for children. If this is so, abuse of children is one of the worst sins which can be committed, and this is a stern warning to paedophiles today.

Next we have instruction on dealing with disputes, which should not be allowed to get out of hand, but settled between brothers. It is interesting to note that when St Benedict drew up a *Rule* for his monks he took similar care that they should have the right relationship with each other, and that disagreements should be quickly settled.

Jesus uses exaggeration or hyperbole in talking about the faith which one should have in the power of God to do the best for us. An example is taken from a deep-rooted tree.

But Wright says that 'faith' in these texts 'is not simply to be understood as a single, miscellaneous religious quality, "virtue" or attribute. It is the distinguishing mark of the true people of YHWH at the time of crisis. It is one of the things, predictably, which will characterize the return from exile.' He quotes the prophets in support of this, especially Habakkuk's words, 'the just shall live by his faith' (Hab. 2:4). Faith therefore is something which should be a feature of the true people of God even when everything seems to be lost. 'What matters is that *faith is a crucial part of the definition of Israel at her time of great crisis.* Jesus' call for "faith" was not merely the offering of a new religious option or dimension. It was a crucial element in the eschatological reconstitution of Israel around himself' (Wright).[46]

Chapter 17:7–10.

These verses are 'a warning against the book-keeping mentality which thinks it can run up a credit balance with God' (Caird). This was a feature of those who lived by the Law and is condemned by Jesus. We can never have a claim against God.

The Journey to Jerusalem Continued: Chapter 17:11ff.

As we have noted before, John's Gospel indicated that Jesus moved up and down Palestine in the course of his ministry. This is not so clear in Luke although there are hints of more than one journey. Here, however, it seems to be the final one to Jerusalem before the Passion.

Chapter 17:11–19. Ten lepers healed.

This cure was not a random miracle but part of the arrival of the kingdom of God which brought healing to all, sinners, outcasts and sick. Following upon what has just been said about faith, we might interpret the words, 'your faith has saved you' as meaning that the lepers have accepted the new order. It was a new relationship with God and his kingdom of grace (Caird). The incident of the thankful Samaritan shows again Luke's interest in non-Jews. A question arises: would the Samaritan have been able to approach a Jewish priest? He certainly would not have been allowed into the temple. Anyway, he had his own Samaritan priests and place of worship!

The Kingdom and Final Disaster: Chapter 17:20–end.[47]

As we have seen throughout, the ministry of Jesus was conducted against the background of the coming of the kingdom of God. The Jewish leaders and people believed this kingdom would come with their final confrontation with the foreign occupying force and their undoubted victory with the support of their God. Jesus taught that the kingdom was already present for those who could read the signs. He could say 'If I by the finger of God cast out demons, no doubt the kingdom of God has come upon you'. This is not enough for the Pharisees, who want further information. Jesus repeats his teaching by saying that the 'kingdom of God is among you'. This is probably better translated 'within your grasp'. If only the Jews had eyes to see and understand, they would know that the kingdom was already present.

It is interesting to note what the apocryphal Gospel of Thomas has to say: 'His disciples said to him, "On what day will the Kingdom come?" He said, "It will not come by expectation. They will not say, 'Look here' or 'Look there' but the Kingdom of the Father is spread out on the earth and people do not see it".' Was this an adaptation within the early Church?

Chapter 17:22–5.

The Son of Man image is found in Daniel 7. Here the Son of Man comes not from heaven to earth but rather from earth to heaven, vindicated after suffering. Thus the 'coming' means both the defeat of the enemies of the true people of God, and the vindication of the true people themselves. Caird says, 'The kingdom and the Son of Man alike will come with the unpredictable ubiquity of a lightning flash, defying all calculation, so that no sentries can be posted to give warning of their approach'. It will be disaster for an unprepared generation.

Chapter 17:26–end.

We now come to a much misunderstood passage. It has often been taken to mean the end of the world. However, both Wright and Caird make the point that the Jews of that time did not think in these terms. Rather, these verses refer to the final disaster when the Romans would destroy Jerusalem, massacre the inhabitants, and end the privileged status which the Jews had had as a people specially chosen by God. It would be more than the end of a chapter but rather the end of a book. The future would lie with a new people of God.

The destruction of Jerusalem, therefore, would seem like the end of the world to the Jews and could be described in words of Old Testament prophets who had foretold this eventuality. The Day of the Lord would not necessarily bring joy and victory to the chosen people, but chaos and punishment if they did not repent (Jeremiah 4:23–6 and Joel 1:16ff.). Then the days of Jerusalem's destruction would be looked upon in terms of a cosmic catastrophe.

So, then, we can interpret this passage as a warning about the coming doom of Jerusalem. We could say that any perceptive person at that time might see the Jews on a roller-coaster ride to destruction and, given the known ruthlessness of the Romans, might have some idea of the coming sufferings. Our Lord was anxious that his followers should not be involved in this battle but should flee.

As Wright notes, 'Jesus did not want his disciples to be caught in the coming destruction. They were not to stay for sentimental or nostalgic reasons, or out of a mistaken sense of national or familial solidarity or loyalty ... they should not stop to pack and get ready, but simply run.' (p. 366) The eagles – presumably the Roman eagles – would gather round the carcass and pick it clean.

Two Parables on Prayer: Chapter 18:1–14.

Chapter 18:1–8. The importunate widow.

At a first reading this seems to be a lesson of persistence in prayer and would apply to any generation of Christians. However, if read in the context of the kingdom of God which Jesus was preaching, there is a deeper meaning. It would apply to the little band of disciples who found themselves standing out against the popular belief that the kingdom would come when God finally backed a military uprising against the Romans. They were in danger of being swept along the road which could only lead to disaster.

There is a lesson here for the modern Christian who stands daily in a torrent of materialism and unbelief. Only a change of life style can save this nation and others from living in a state of confrontation with each other which, with our deadly weapons of destruction, could lead to a total disaster far greater than the fall of Jerusalem. Yet the nation rushes on its downward path, trusting perhaps that the arrival of a new millennium will somehow give it a more hopeful future. It is a situation not dissimilar to the one in Our Lord's day.

So, we may read this parable of the widow as teaching that God would vindicate his elect who cry to him day and night. This vindicated elect would not be those who were the leaders of Israel's national life, but those who cried incessantly to their God for vindication without claiming that they were righteous keepers of the Law.

Chapter 18:9–14.

This leads on to the next parable or story of two men who went into the temple to pray. They could not have been more different: one was a self-righteous Pharisee, and the other a tax-collector, who was an outcast as far as Jewish religion was concerned. As Caird notes, although they both went to pray, only one did so. Prayer must be directed to God, but the Pharisee was only interested in himself. All his verbs are in the first person – 'I'. The tax-collector, on the other hand, fixed his attention on God and knew himself to be a sinner. He was the one who went away justified or vindicated.

We have in this parable another guide to what the gospel was all about. The Pharisees' emphasis on merit and legal observance was clean contrary to the teaching of

Jesus about the change of heart which was necessary before the kingdom of God could come.

So the followers of Jesus should be humble and throw themselves on God's compassion. They would be the forgiven ones and would be exalted in the future when Israel's God finally acted. Wright says that Luke's ending to this discourse comes in chapter 21. The disciples 'must not allow their concentration to wander, must not settle down and while away their lives (21:34-6). They must be waiting to stand before the "son of man" to share in his vindication.'

Chapter 18:15-17. Jesus and children.

The writer of an article in a modern newspaper has regretted that we have so little information about the person of Christ. He writes that although we may claim that the world has been radically changed by Christ, we do not know what he was like. Yet for those who study the gospels carefully, much can be learnt. We have already seen how Jesus could move easily among women and used them in his work without creating scandal. In these verses and elsewhere, we can learn about his relationship with the young. Children do not take to strangers, but they obviously trusted Jesus. This trust was also essential for all who were working for the kingdom of God.

Teaching on Possessions. Chapter 18:18-27.

The question whether Jesus taught that his followers should give up all to follow him has been debated through the ages, and in these verses we seem to come to the last word on the subject. For those who believe that Jesus preached the end of the world order, it has seemed logical that earthly possessions should have no value for the future and should be given away. If, however, we have followed Luke carefully, we may conclude that Jesus was not predicting the end of the world but was seeking to change his nation's way of life for the establishment of his

Father's kingdom in *this* world. Therefore we may have to modify our ideas about this particular passage.

First, something must be said about the Jewish attitude toward riches and possessions. Some Jews, following Deuteronomy and some of the psalms, believed that wealth was the sign of God's favour. So the disciples were astonished when Jesus taught that rich people would have difficulty in entering the kingdom (25-6) because they assumed that the rich would be part of it. Jesus, however, was only saying that the rich were not automatically within the covenant but could be outside it. We have the examples of men like Zacchaeus and Joseph of Arimathea, who became followers of Jesus but who kept at least some of their possessions.

We must also understand that in Our Lord's day, not only for Jews but for other Middle Eastern people, land was the most basic possession and the most precious thing a man could leave to his children. To give up one's wealth was as drastic as to abandon family loyalties. As Wright notes, family and property were not for the ancient Jew what they are to our modern western world. Both carried religious and cultural significance far beyond personal identity and security. Jesus issued a challenge to his followers: to be loyal to his kingdom-agenda; they would have to be prepared to renounce family and possessions, even though these might come from God.

We may now return to the ruler who is the subject of these verses and his question: What must I do to inherit eternal life? Wright warns us against thinking that it is like a modern question: What must I do to go to heaven when I die? The ruler (Matthew calls him young) wants to know what he needs to do to have a share in the age to come when God will vindicate his truly faithful people. As Caird puts it: 'he [had] supposed that entry to the kingdom was by competitive examination. He had passed elementary religion to his own satisfaction', and wanted to move on to a more advanced stage. The Law or Torah was the criterion which decided on a place in the coming age.

The ruler was not satisfied, possibly because Jesus had quoted only some of the commandments. Jesus gives a firm answer: sell all and give to the poor. We are not told that Jesus gave this answer regularly, although he often demands sacrifice from his followers. Here, however, Jesus sees that the ruler is ready to move into a world governed not by law-keeping but by complete allegiance to himself. As Wright puts it: 'instead of being under Torah, the summons was now to be under Jesus'. This was too much and the ruler went sorrowfully away.

What then was expected of other followers who did not receive such a drastic command? The answer might be found in Acts 4:35. 'Distribution was made to each one as he had *need'* – not necessarily what he wanted! Jesus saw the dangers of the system of family and property ownership. Defence of it was driving the Jews into a war they could not win. It was like a general who had not calculated sufficiently whether he had enough troops to meet an enemy.

Chapter 18:28–30.

Peter is encouraged by the conversation with the ruler and asks what will be the reward for those who had already made great sacrifices. As Caird notes: 'Jesus promises that those who have left home and family for the service of the kingdom will find themselves caring for a far bigger family than the one they left, before ever they reach the eternal life of the age to come.'

Chapter 18:31–4.

There follows a further warning about the trials which Jesus is walking into, but which will end in triumph. Understandably this was beyond the disciples' comprehension. As we have seen earlier, this was the kind of warning that any rebel leader might give to his followers.

Jesus knew that through his ministry he was bringing the power and effect of God to bear on many lives in need of healing and forgiveness. He also knew that he had to go

to Jerusalem, because only there could a decision be made
by the authorities as to whether he was truly a teacher of
God's word.

Chapter 18:35–43. A blind beggar in Jericho.

Luke tells us (9:51) that Jesus and his followers had set out
on the journey south through Samaria. So he would have
been following the *Via Maris*, or coastal trade route which
would have brought him to Jerusalem via Lod and
Emmaus. Yet Luke tells us that the party had now come to
Jericho, which was a long way off course and fifteen miles
steeply downhill from the capital. If, however, they had
travelled south along the course of the Jordan valley this
would have brought them to Jericho. Maybe Luke is
mixing up two separate journeys – we know from John's
Gospel that Jesus went south from Galilee more than once.

Jericho is situated close to the barren and arid terrain of
the Dead Sea, but because it has an abundant supply of
water it is very fertile and plants grow easily there. For
this reason it has been settled without a break for thou-
sands of years. A tourist today walks into a profusion of
fruit and vegetables. With such wealth, it would have been
a profitable centre for a tax-collector like Zacchaeus.

First, however, we meet in contrast a blind beggar who,
no doubt informed by the crowd about the important
visitor, cries out for help from the 'Son of David'. This is
the only occasion in the Gospels where this title is used
and could have reflected not the beggar's private belief
but that of Jesus' fellow pilgrims (see 19:38). Jesus,
however, will not only heal the man, who is really only
interested in begging, but makes it an occasion for a lesson
in faith – a recognition that Israel's God is active in and
through himself.

Chapter 19:1–10. Zacchaeus.

We do not know what prompted this man to take such an
undignified move to see Jesus. He might well have wanted
to escape from his unpopular profession of tax-collector,

which had isolated him within the community. Anyway, Jesus noticed him and invited himself into his house. This provoked hostility, because he had become the guest of a sinner, but Jesus had caused a generous conversion. If Zacchaeus did not give up all his possessions, he did share them with the needy. This prompted Jesus to include him in the membership of the renewed people of the covenant God, which caused scandal because, on his own authority, he declared Zacchaeus to be a true son of Abraham.

Chapter 19:11–28. The Parable/Story of the Pounds.

Jesus is here probably illustrating his teaching with political incidents which had taken place in AD 6. At the death of Herod, Archelaus went to Rome to get Caesar's consent to his succession. His Jewish subjects did not like him and sent a rival deputation to ask that Archelaus should not be appointed. However, Archelaus was successful, returned home and punished his enemies. These were events which would have been remembered by Jesus' audience in AD 30. They were unlikely to be of similar interest to the early Church. We should therefore modify Caird's statement that the parable was told as a warning to those who expected an imminent return of Christ to bring in the final consummation of his kingdom and that it was specially directed toward the first Christians.[48] As Wright notes, it is straining probability too far to think of Jesus trying to explain to people who had not grasped the fact of his imminent death, that there would follow an indeterminate period, after which he would return in some spectacular fashion for which nothing in their tradition had prepared them.

Luke tells the story because Jesus and his followers were approaching Jerusalem and there was high expectation that the kingdom was near. And so it was, but not in the way the Jews expected. As Wright says, in most parables about a king and his subjects or a master and his servants, the king or master stands for Israel's God and the subjects or servants stand for Israel and her leaders. Jews were used to thinking of their relationship with their God as that between a lord and his 'slaves'.

So the idea of a king returning after a long absence would fit in with the return of YHWH to Sion. This was already a belief of some contemporary Jews and had been emphasized by Jesus throughout his teaching ministry. God was about to return to his people, but what would he find? Jesus could see his journey to Jerusalem as a dress rehearsal for the return of God to his people. So he weeps over the sad state of religion he finds in the city, and creates a disturbance in the temple. By doing this he acts dramatically and symbolically the judgement of YHWH on his rebel people. As Wright notes, he was not content like the Essenes to wage war on the religious system by words from afar but took his message into the heart of the city. He also was not satisfied with the place the Torah or Law held in the preparation of his people for the arrival of the kingdom. This was like the servant who buried his lord's money.

When, therefore, this parable is placed within Our Lord's actual ministry and not in a future Christian community, it becomes a warning about the judgement which would come upon those who had refused to accept what God had been doing in the ministry of his Son. This is another example of the warning message which Jesus gave in similar parables about masters returning to find servants in different stages of readiness. In the present parable of the pounds, 'Jesus implies an analogy between those who rejected Archelaus a generation earlier and those who, in his own day, prefer their dreams of national independence to the coming of the true king' (Wright). Just as the king came from Rome and punished those who rejected him, so judgement was coming upon those who did not receive the kingdom which Jesus preached. Had not the prophets foretold that the day of the Lord might be woe and not joy?

As we have learnt earlier, parables rarely had a simple explanation, but could contain explosive material. This would seem to be the case with the story of the pounds.

PRELUDE TO THE PASSION

Why Did Jesus Die?

This is a question which has been continuously debated for much of Christian history. Were the Jews responsible or the Romans? Or was it some kind of tragic accident? Was it the result of the confluence of two different cultures in which Jesus became the unfortunate victim of misunderstanding?

The Jewish Charge.

If we have followed the course of Jesus' ministry so far we may well come to the conclusion that his trial and death were no unrelated ending. Throughout the gospel narrative we have seen Jesus and the Jewish authorities on entirely different missions. As we noted (pp. 84ff.) there were two battle lines drawn up. Both, it is true, had the coming of the kingdom of God in their sights, but with radically opposite conceptions about what this would involve. The Jews were intent on military action to clear the foreign occupier from their land, and for this they relied on a faithful keeping of the Law and the centrality of temple worship. This would ensure that God would intervene in a future uprising, bring in a new age for those who had faithfully kept the Law, and rule in person at last from the temple. For the rest of God's people there would be little hope in a coming judgement.

Jesus preached that any future kingdom would have little hope of permanence unless the Jewish people had a change of heart and adopted a life style which demanded love and the salvation of all his Father's creation. For this, Satan or the power of evil had to be defeated first, and Jesus undertook this battle, pushing him further and further back by healing the sick, raising the dead, forgiving sins and correcting false teaching. This he did in the name of and through the authority of his Father in heaven.

He did not hesitate to rewrite the Law and sideline the temple. This involved him in violent debate, shown most clearly in John's Gospel where we learn that confrontation ended in attempts to stone him to death (John 7:30; 8:59).

The Jews did not understand what Jesus was doing. He seemed to pose no threat either to the Jewish or the Roman government. Yet he was performing signs, people might be led away after him, the temple and national life were at risk. In addition, Jesus could well be committing blasphemy by his claim to be acting with the authority of God. In fact, there is evidence from a later Jewish document that 'Jesus was hanged on the eve of the Passover' because he practised sorcery and enticed and led Israel astray. In other words Jesus died because of crimes punishable by death in Jewish law, especially that found in Deuteronomy 13, as interpreted by later rabbis.

The Roman Charge.

The involvement of Pilate was a more straightforward matter, once Pilate's character is known. Roman justice was respected throughout the ancient world, but it could go wrong in the hands of bad administrators. Crucifixion was a means of execution mostly for those who had shown defiance against the sovereignty of Rome and Caesar. Rebel leaders were crucified as a clear and frightening symbolic act. So it might be said that Jesus was put to death as a rebel leader. Yet if we understand correctly the gospel account, Pilate was by no means certain that Jesus offered any threat to his authority.

There was no reason why Pilate could have learnt about the background of this Jewish teacher. The Romans, according to Sanders, kept a low profile throughout Palestine and the only damaging report about Jesus might have been that he had trained a number of followers in Galilee and sent them out to support his work. There has been a tendency to whitewash Pilate and to put the blame entirely on the Jewish authorities. However, independent evidence shows Pilate to have been neither a competent nor a distinguished official. He appeared scared that any mismanagement might be reported back to Tiberius. He had already given way when a delegation threatened to appeal to Rome when he caused offence by putting golden shields in the Herodian palace. Philo, a first-century author, writes: 'He feared that if they actually sent an embassy, they would expose the rest of his conduct as governor by stating in full the briberies, the insults, the robberies, the outrages and wanton injustices, the executions without trial constantly repeated, the ceaseless and supremely grievous cruelty'. Philo may be exaggerating, but he is in part supported by Josephus, the Jewish historian turned Roman sympathizer, who shows Pilate as a brutal and insensitive ruler. The political situation in Rome was uncertain because at that time Tiberius had become a thoroughly unreliable figure. The threat, therefore, of the chief priests, that if he did not do what they wanted, he would not be a friend of Caesar (John 19:12) probably made Pilate give way. Pilate was caught between his desire not to do what his Jewish subjects wanted and his fear of what Tiberius would think if the news leaked out.

So it is difficult to acquit Pilate of the blame for sending Jesus to his death. He was the governor and could have released Jesus if he had been strong enough. Instead he contemptuously washed his hands, and pretended that he could evade responsibility for something which lay entirely within his power. Nevertheless, the situation would never have arisen if the chief priests had not demanded the death penalty.

The Predictions of Jesus.

We have read in earlier chapters that Jesus warned his disciples that he would be arrested, flogged and be put to death (9:22) and this warning was repeated in 18:32. Given the confrontations Jesus had almost daily with the religious authorities about his teaching, he must have known what lay ahead for him. Had not the prophets of old suffered because they dared to give unpopular warnings? As was noted earlier, John's gospel described vividly the fierce daily battle which Jesus had with the authorities and, given that attempts had already been made to kill him by stoning, it was inevitable that they would in time have their way. We may therefore assume that when Jesus finally went up to Jerusalem, he went to die. As Wright points out, a key to Our Lord's intention may be found in his words at the Last Supper.

To Sum Up.

Jesus was sent to the Roman governor because:

1. the Jewish authorities saw him as a false prophet, leading Israel astray
2. his action in the temple was seen as a blow against the central symbol of national life
3. as some sort of Messiah, he could be the focal point of a revolutionary movement
4. he was seen as a political nuisance who might alienate the Romans
5. he pleaded guilty to charges of blasphemy by claiming a special relationship with God.

ENTRY INTO JERUSALEM: CHAPTER 19:28–48.

We left Jesus and his followers in Jericho, and this would have meant a fifteen-mile walk uphill to the Mount of Olives and then into Jerusalem. Pilgrims still stop within sight of the city and sing Psalm 122:1:

> I was glad when they said unto me,
> Let us go into the house of the Lord.
> Our feet shall stand within thy gates, O Jerusalem.

The entry and all that followed was full of symbolism for those living in Israel and who knew their Old Testament. Caird calls it, The Royal Visit, and certainly it has all the trappings of a king's procession. There is also more than an echo of the First Book of the Maccabees when Judas Maccabaeus, having defeated the Greek enemy, entered Jerusalem, cleansed the temple and restored true worship. Jesus was performing Maccabaean actions, though with radical differences, according to Wright. He continues by saying that the High Priestly party, which had a connection with the Hasmonean (Maccabaean) dynasty, would have found Jesus' action in the temple as threatening.

Jesus' entry followed faithfully the prophecy of Zechariah 9:9:

Rejoice greatly, O daughter Sion!
Shout aloud, O daughter Jerusalem!
Lo, your king comes to you: triumphant and victorious
    is he,
humble and riding on a donkey,
on a colt, the foal of a donkey.

So Jesus sends two disciples to bring a colt with the message, 'The lord or master has need of it.' As one commentator notes, Jesus is here laying a claim to the animal, and I am tempted to add that it might have been given to him for his use on a previous visit to the city.

So Jesus rides into the city to the accompaniment of words from Ps. 118:26 said over pilgrims coming to a festival, Blessings on him who comes in the name of the Lord. Luke adds the words, *'as king'*. The enthusiasm of the crowd is enough to offend the Pharisees.

Chapter 19:41–4.

The heart of the tragedy is summed up in the word, *'visitation'*. Israel had for so long waited for a royal visit from their God. Now when it comes in the person of Jesus, they

are not ready for it, and Jesus describes how the tragedy
would end.

It has been said by some commentators that Luke is
following the description of the actual fall of Jerusalem in
AD 70 by Josephus, which would have given a late date to
his gospel, but Wright points out that there are many striking differences. Some of his graphic details find no
mention in the synoptic gospels. It is better to regard the
details of the city's destruction as following biblical
prophecy. Anyway, the method employed by the Roman
army to destroy a town or city was well known, as the
inhabitants of Sepphoris had cause to remember.

Chapter 19:45–6. The cleansing of the temple.

It has been suggested that by driving out the traders and
scattering the money of the moneychangers, Jesus was
causing a temporary disruption of the sacrificial system
because worshippers would be unable to buy animals.
This might be seen as a symbol of the final destruction of
the temple system in AD 70.

Although Judas Maccabaeus believed there was a future
for a reformed temple worship, throughout the gospels
Jesus had shown that he could not foresee a place in the
kingdom of God for it at all. It was too badly compromised
by corruption. Yet in Jewish expectation the temple would
take a crucial place in the coming new age and their God
would rule in person from it. Any attack on it, therefore,
could be seen as blasphemy.

John alone puts the cleansing of the temple at the beginning of his Gospel and follows it with considerable teaching. The future temple would be identified with Jesus
himself after the resurrection. Unlike John, the other three
gospels record only one visit of Jesus to Jerusalem and so
would need to place the temple incident toward the end.
Either way, it clearly played a vital part in the condemna-
tion of Jesus, and his words about the temple's destruction
were thrown back at him after his arrest and during his
crucifixion. If in the thought of the synoptists the cleansing

of the temple was the final cause for the death of Jesus, it should be said that John sees this in the raising of Lazarus.

Chapter 19:47–8. The gathering clouds.

The religious authorities have decided that Jesus must be put out of the way, but must wait until he is not surrounded by the enthusiasm of the crowd. Compare these verses with John 11:47–57.

Question Time for the King.

Today a person who hits the headlines faces interviews by the media. Some questions are easily answered, but others have to be more discreetly handled. This was the case with Jesus as he faced a barrage of awkward questions, and he left his questioners to come to their own conclusions.

Chapter 20:1–8. A question of authority.

Jesus has already challenged features of national life, and now has attacked the temple system. What right has he to do this? Jesus at this stage could have disclosed his true identity as saviour or Messiah, but this might have over-excited the crowd and brought down the full forces of law and order on them. So he deals with the question in the same way as he had dealt with the Baptist's inquiry. 'Are you he who should come or do we look for another?' Jesus might have said, 'Yes, I am the Messiah', but this could have alerted Herod. So he reminds John about the signs he has given – the deaf hear, the blind see, the dead are raised, etc. – and leaves him to come to his own conclusion.

So now Jesus turns aside the question of the religious authorities by directing them to the Baptist. John was a prophet, the greatest who had ever lived. Malachi had spoken about the last prophet who would come before the final great day had dawned. If John was the last of the preparatory prophets, where are we now? There is a clear answer. The one who is least in the kingdom is greater than John, and Jesus is preaching the arrival of that kingdom. His action in the temple was carried out because he was the one to whom John had pointed. If John is the last in the line of prophets, after him comes the king.

Chapter 20:9–18. The wicked tenants and the stone.

The early Church and later generations of Christians have had little difficulty in applying this parable to the treatment the Lord received at the hands of his fellow countrymen. We might note that in Luke the son was taken out of the vineyard and killed, which could be an indication of what happened at the crucifixion: Jesus was executed outside the city walls.

For a Jewish audience, there could have been a further interpretation. As Caird writes, any Jew who heard this story would have been reminded of Isaiah's parable of the vineyard (5:1–7). Here the vineyard represented Israel, and it was inevitable that the Jewish authorities would have recognized that Jesus was telling the story against them.

Wright notes that the parable follows what had been said about the Baptist. In one sense Jesus was the last of the prophets looking for fruit from the vineyard, in another John was the last in the line and after the messenger comes the son. Wright continues by saying that since 2 Samuel 7 was used in the first century as a reference to the Messiah and his role in building the temple, the natural reading of the parable is that the final messenger, bringing the last of the prophetic warnings, is also different in kind. He is the Messiah.[50]

Isaiah's parable of the vineyard ends with its destruction because it failed to produce fruit. Psalm 80 also refers to the sad state of the vine which God had brought out of Egypt. Jesus could be reviving this theme, suggesting that just as Isaiah prophesied the destruction of the temple in his day, so he was foretelling its destruction in his age. So his cleansing of the temple was a symbol of what was about to happen. In both Isaiah's and Jesus' case prophecy came true.

This leads on to the quotation from Psalm 118 about the stone which the builders rejected having become the main cornerstone. At first sight this seems out of place, but the apocryphal gospel of Thomas makes it follow the parable of the wicked tenants. Since the psalm was used by those going in procession to the temple, we may understand why Jesus chose that time for his symbolic act of cleansing, and also made a cryptic remark about the rebuilding of a new kind of temple: the rejected stone would become the chief cornerstone. Wright links all this with texts from the Old Testament. Isaiah talks about God laying in Sion

> a foundation stone, a tested stone,
> a precious cornerstone, a sure foundation (28:16).

In 8:14 Isaiah speaks about God or YHWH himself becoming

> a sanctuary, a stone one strikes against; for both houses of Israel he will become a rock one stumbles over – a trap and a snare for the inhabitants of Jerusalem.

Zechariah 4:7–10 refers to the rebuilding programme after the return from Babylon. The passage becomes even more interesting when it is realized that the Hebrew for stone was *eben* and the word for son was *ben*. As Wright notes, the pun might not have escaped the notice of some. So the rejected son in the parable becomes the messianic stone rejected by the builders but takes its chief place in the building. Such thinking might well be understood by Jesus and his hearers though not by later writers of the early Church – yet it was included by Luke!

Chapter 20:19–26. The problem of paying taxes.

As was noted earlier, the decision by religious leaders to silence Jesus was not taken at the last minute. The chief difficulty was his support among the people. John 11:47 is a parallel passage. Meanwhile questions were put to Jesus to find out where he stood on major issues of the day, first on the payment of taxes to Caesar.

In modern times there has been much debate about the unity of nations in the west and a common currency. This was no problem in the first century AD, for the Pax Romana, established by Augustus Caesar and continued by his successor Tiberius, had brought in a period of relative peace and prosperity for the civilized Mediterranean world, albeit by military conquests. This brought several advantages, not least in the economy and in communications. The cost of administering the empire was met by taxes, and this was paid in Roman coinage, silver denarii, stamped with the image of Caesar. The fact that he had been declared a god was no problem to most nations, but it was of grave concern for the Jews who had a law against such images. Rebel leaders made this an important issue, and in deference to Jewish scruples a copper coin without the image was minted for Palestine. It was not always used, and the silver denarius was widely circulated. Jesus would have known this, and when he asked for a silver coin, it was readily produced. This showed the dishonesty of his questioners who were already compromising with the occupying power. By accepting the Roman coinage and with it the benefits conferred by Rome in the way of economic stability and good order, these Jews had already answered their own questions but there was nothing unreasonable in this, as Jesus seems to indicate. Caesar was carrying out his God-given function of providing a framework of order for the common life of man and had a right to claim his due. It was another matter if Caesar should claim what belongs only to God, the unconditional allegiance of men. Jesus therefore adds further teaching by reminding his questioners of their duty to obey God, and that meant accepting the Messiah he had sent.

Wright adds the thought that, seeking to overthrow Caesar in the name of YHWH and the Torah, the revolutionaries were using Caesar's own weapons. They were the real compromisers. God acted differently.

Chapter 20:27–38. A question on marriage.

Again this was no trick question but a matter of difference about the afterlife. The Sadducees did not believe in a resurrection, and so it was important for them to do well in this world and to be able to pass on their success to the next generation. So they quote an example of desperate attempts of seven brothers to create an heir by marrying the same woman, and then tried to show how this made a belief in an afterlife absurd.

Pharisees, on the other hand, tended to think of resurrection as being a return to a carnal life on a grander scale. Jesus answers both, first by showing that a belief in the afterlife was implicit in the Torah, so the Sadducees were wrong. At the same time he teaches that the afterlife is more than a continuation of this present life with all its imperfections and desires.

Chapter 20:41–4. A question about David.

As Wright notes, Jesus now puts a royal riddle to his questioners; Wright confesses that a modern mind might not understand its significance. First, we should know that Jesus held the first-century belief that David had written Psalm 110 (it was probably written long after David's time, but this does not affect the thrust of the argument). The 'Lord' refers to God, while 'my lord' for the author of the psalm, is the king. In other words, the psalm was about the king rather than by him.

Jesus is not denying his Davidic lineage, which seems to have been accepted. Rather, he is using Psalm 110, which was assumed to be about the Messiah, to teach that Jews must revise their idea of this figure who is greater than popular belief.

But how much greater? If we follow the psalm further we shall find ourselves in another dimension altogether, for it refers to the enthronement of the Messiah, to his successful battle against the kings of the earth, and to being a priest for ever after the order of Melchizedek. As Wright notes, this idea of enthronement belongs to a number of texts in which a figure, possible messianic, is enthroned beside YHWH himself. A Qumran fragment suggests that the one who is so enthroned may have been the eschatological priest-teacher. So the Jews had to raise their ideas about the nature of a coming Messiah.[51]

Since this question is being asked within the temple, we might ask if Jesus is using it to explain his cleansing action. As Malachi had prophesied:

> Suddenly the Lord will come to his temple . . .
> Who can endure the day of his coming? Who shall
>   stand firm when he appears?
> He is like a refiner's fire, like a fuller's soap;
> he will take his seat, testing and purifying;
> he will purify the Levites and refine them like gold
>   and silver (3:1–4)

Also, as a priest after the order of Melchizedek, the Messiah might supersede the existing high priestly regime. So could the action of Jesus be seen as a preliminary confrontation with a corrupt priestly system? Jesus showed authority not merely as David's son but as his Lord.

Finally, the psalm envisages a judge who will pronounce judgement on YHWH's enemies. This had so far been taken to mean foreigners, but Jesus had already indicated that the real enemies were nearer to hand.

Chapter 20:45 — 21:4. The rich and the poor.

The theme of these verses seems to be 'widows'. Prosperous doctors of the law 'prey upon' (a better translation than 'devour') the property of widows, and are condemned by Jesus. Wealth was of great importance in Jewish society, and almsgiving could be done without much sacrifice. On the other hand, even a small offering was costly to a poor widow, and Jesus commends it. This is yet another example of the teaching of Jesus on possessions.

Judgement Day: Chapter 21:5–end.

Jesus has already spoken about a coming disaster (17:22ff.). He now repeats his prophecy and warns of further horrors and what action his followers should take. It has been the custom in the Christian Church to understand the Lord's words as referring to the end of the world, but it should be stated again that in Judaism there was no place for such a catastrophe. As Wright notes,'no Jews whose opinions are known to us thought that their god was about to bring the space-time world, including land and temple, to a sudden end'. Such a disaster therefore must be thought of as happening within history. There was plenty of imagery in the Old Testament about what was called the Day of the Lord. In Isaiah we find this description:

> The day of the Lord is coming,
> that cruel day and fierce anger,
> to reduce the earth to desolation
> and destroy all the wicked there.
> The stars of heaven in their constellations
> will give no light,
> and the sun will be dark at its rising,
> and the moon will not shed its light (13:9–10)

> All the hosts of heaven will crumble into nothing,
> the heavens will be rolled up like a scroll,
> all their host fade away (34:4).

The Book of Zephaniah also has vivid warnings about the Day of the Lord. The Book of Daniel had great influence in Jewish thinking about a final judgement of which the faithful law-keeper should have no fear. A new handbook to the Bible summarizes what Jews of Jesus' day believed about this phenomenon:

> History moves to a purpose under the control of God:
> the calculation of times and seasons is revealed

History is moving to a final climax when the enemies of
God and Israel will be defeated

Cosmic powers as well as earthly enemies pit themselves against God and the people of faith but they
are defeated

The faithful people of God will be rewarded – this
means that God has the power to restore them to life
after death

Suffering and trouble in the present are birth pangs of a
new age in which the Messiah will come and rule

The coming kingdom and the reward of the faithful
(and the punishment of the wicked) are described.[52]

All this forms Jewish apocalyptic and is sometimes
disguised in code – for example in Daniel. Jesus, therefore,
had a powerful background for his teaching about the
future. The great difference of course is the qualification
for future blessedness.

The Son of Man.

There was, therefore, much Old Testament imagery to
describe Judgement Day and Jesus uses some of it in his
teaching in the temple. He had already taught that those
who expected to be justified might find themselves shut
out of the coming kingdom of God, and that unlikely
people might enter.

Jesus mentions the 'coming of the Son of Man', and this
phrase over the years has been the subject of much speculation. At one time it was thought that this referred to the
Messiah who would come to carry out the final judgement, but attention has in recent years been directed at the
book of Daniel, which was full of apocalyptic significance.
Josephus writes that chapters 2, 7 and 9 more than
anything else incited the Jews to revolt. As we have seen
earlier in this book, Daniel 2 named four foreign occupations before God would be ready to bring in his kingdom,
and the Romans were the last. It should be noted that the
Book of Daniel, although dealing with the exile in

Babylon, was probably written much later when the Jews were fighting desperately against the third invader, the Greeks, with many acts of heroism. In Daniel 7 we read of a vision in which the writer saw a fight against a number of beasts and then writes: 'I was still watching in visions in the night and I saw one like a son of man coming with the clouds of heaven; he approached the Ancient of Days and was presented to him. Sovereignty and kingly glory were given to him ...'(13–15). Professor Moule comments that he believed Jesus did refer to Daniel 7, speaking of *the* Son of Man, and that he used Daniel's human figure not primarily as a title so much as a symbol for the vocation to victory through obedience and martyrdom to which he was called, and to which he summoned his followers (so that they would constitute 'the people of the saints of the Most High ...'). (*NewTestament Studies*, Vol. 41, 1995.)

Wright supports this interpretation and says that the 'coming of the son of man' does not refer to the *parousia* in the modern and popular sense of a human figure travelling downwards toward the earth on actual clouds, nor does the phrase refer to a superhuman figure. He continues by saying that 'coming' (Greek *erchomenon*) could be understood as the son of man coming *from* earth *to* heaven before the Ancient of Days, and that he comes vindicated after suffering. As Wright adds, 'the Danielic story always was one of vindication and exaltation, and was retold as such in the first century. The 'coming of the son of man' is thus good first-century metaphorical language for two things: the defeat of the enemies of the true people of god and the vindication of the true people themselves.' It is in this connection that Daniel 9 should be read (op. cit. p. 361).

Meanwhile Jesus' faithful followers should take care not to be caught in the coming disaster. Rather should they strengthen themselves for the task of witness which would follow the fall of Jerusalem.

THE PASSION NARRATIVE

Prelude to the Trials: Chapter 2:1–6.

There is now support for recognizing that the true trial of
Jesus took place some weeks before the actual arrest of
Jesus. John Robinson, commenting on John 11:45–53, says
that here we have a formally-convened meeting of the
Sanhedrin at which they 'resolved' or 'passed a resolution'
that Jesus should be put to death and at which he is
publicly declared a wanted man. For John continues, 'the
chief priests and the Pharisees had given orders that any
one who knew where he was should give information, so
that they might arrest him.' Robinson is supported by
Bammel who points out that this passage is full of quasi-
technical terms. 'To give orders' describes the issue of a
writ. John 11:56 describes the search which takes place to
find out the whereabouts of a fugitive, and 'anyone who
knew where he was should give information' denotes the
denunciation (*menuein* in Greek) of a person named in the
writ. Taken together the terms can easily be considered as
indicating the different stages of a proscription. Bammel
adds that this was the action undertaken against those
who had not been present at the original indictment. The
word *menuein* was the technical word used for an
informer, and Joseph recalls the provision of the Mosaic
law that if a murderer cannot be found 'let them make dili-
gent search for the culprit, offering rewards for information'. That the warrant was accompanied by a reward 'for
information leading to his arrest' is not stated in any of the
Gospels but would provide an entirely probable background for Judas's action.

Robinson remarks that the significance of John 11:47–57
has received little notice. He summarizes three distinctive
features:

1) We have a picture of the prosecution of Jesus which
   makes the legal proceedings begin a considerable time

before the crucifixion. This is in line with extraneous rabbinic writings which said: On the eve of the Passover Yeshu was hanged. For forty days before the execution took place, a herald went forth and cried, 'He is going forth to be stoned because he practised sorcery and enticed Israel to apostasy. Anyone who can say anything in his favour, let him come forward and plead on his behalf.' But since nothing was brought forward in his favour, he was hanged on the eve of the Passover.[53]

This presupposes a considerable delay in Jesus' case between incrimination and execution. This was due to the fact that the Jewish authorities could not lay hands on him. However, the decision that Jesus was guilty had been made, and he had merely to be confronted with the charge and asked if he had anything to say in his defence.

2) It should be noted that legal proceedings were started and carried out entirely by the Jews. At this stage the proceedings lie entirely in the hands of the Jewish supreme court, which quite legally issues the warrant for the arrest, observing the proper procedural delay, though the implication is that the man is already guilty until proved otherwise.

3) We should also note the part played by Caiaphas, who had great experience in dealings with matters of expediency. He was known to have a working relationship with Pilate.

4) Jesus no longer went about publicly but withdrew to a country district (John 11:54).

In the light of all this, it is possible to understand that Luke (22:1–2) is also drawing attention to an early trial and also (3–6) how Judas fits into the picture as an important informer. We do not know if he was after the money or had a deeper reason for betraying his master. Certainly the fracas in the temple and the hostile questioning which followed may have been a severe test of loyalty.

The Last Supper. Chapter 22:14ff.

If, as John says, Jesus retreated to a country area on the edge of Jerusalem after the Lazarus episode he now returns to the city for, as he had said, 'it is unthinkable for a prophet to meet his death anywhere but in Jerusalem' (13:34), and he was the greatest and the last of the prophets. The fact that he could give directions for booking accommodation indicates once more that this was not the first time he had visited the south.

Jesus' ministry had always been carried out within the history and symbolism of his people, and there was no greater symbol than that of the Passover celebration. He was therefore about to use Israel's occasion for celebrating a great deliverance in the past and hope for the future to give a means of anticipating an even greater deliverance. The modern reader, however, may need a short diversion here to understand the importance which the family evening meal had for first-century Jews – and still has. For in the western world today fewer and fewer families sit down together for a meal, even on Sunday, and the younger generations especially grab a quick snack before getting on with other concerns. Certainly the idea of using meal times for a religious purpose has disappeared, and rarely is there even a grace before food.

Other ages have treated food differently. For the Jews the evening meal has been an occasion for thanking God for his goodness to his people throughout history, and an extended grace or blessing is said by the head of the family. One such prayer is: 'Blessed are you, Lord our God, King of the universe, God our father, our king, our creator and redeemer, good and beneficent king, who day by day is concerned to benefit us in many ways, and himself will increase us for ever in grace and kindness and spirit and mercy and every good thing.' At the Passover meal there was special ceremonial with prayers and psalms. The exodus from Egypt many centuries before was remembered and rehearsed. Families dressed as if for a journey, unleavened bread was used and the main dish was lamb. It was in fact more than just remembering what had happened originally. *Remember* and *memorial* in Biblical terms meant bringing something back from the past and making it live in the present. Each family acted as if they were about to be delivered from bondage in Egypt, and they looked forward to the time when God would save them again from foreign masters. On Passover night the head of the family reminded the gathering of the details when 'Israel came out of Egypt'. This was then celebrated with a meal and cups of wine.

Jesus at the Last Supper took over the Passover celebration and gave it a new meaning. The Jews were looking forward to a new exodus when God would return and rule from his temple. Jesus used the meal to bring his own kingdom-movement to its climax. In this way he indicated that the new exodus with all its implications was happening through himself. As some scholars have noted, there is a strong connection between Jesus' action in cleansing the temple, and the Last Supper. If these are taken together, Jesus is teaching that he intends to replace the temple as a focal point of Jewish religion with his own special meal. Despite some difference of wording in the three gospel accounts, it is clear that Jesus 'identified the bread with his own body, and the wine with his own blood, and that he spoke about these in language which echoed the context of Passover, sacrifice, and covenant which the meal must have already possessed' (Wright). Jesus also indicated that this meal was the last he would share before the kingdom arrived. The idea of the blood of the covenant which appears in both Matthew and Mark is found in the Old Testament. In Exodus 24:8 Moses established the first covenant with the people at Mount Sinai, and in Zechariah 9:9–11 there is a significant passage which follows the well-known words about rejoicing because the king comes triumphant and humble, riding on a donkey ... the passage ends: 'As for you also, because of the blood of my covenant with you, I will set your prisoners free from the waterless pit'. Zechariah, like Daniel, provides important background for understanding the vocation of the Messiah especially as he approaches his final days. As Wright says, 'there should be no doubt but that Jesus intended to say, with all the power of symbolic drama and narrative, that he was shortly to die, and that his death was to be seen within the context of the larger story of God's redemption of Israel.'

Two further lessons may be drawn from the institution of the Last Supper. If we follow what was said earlier about the meaning of the phrase, son of man, who goes from earth upward to the Ancient of Days as representative of those who had suffered for the true faith, then we may conclude that those who take part in the Eucharist may also be offered with the son of man who has entered the Holy of Holies, an idea which is developed in the Letter to the Hebrews.

Then we might note that when the Last Supper is repeated within the Eucharist, God is responsible for the whole action. For the first part of the service contains readings which tell us what God has done for his people throughout history, especially in his Son Jesus Christ. This should make us want to respond with thanksgiving and worship, but since we have nothing worthy to offer, God makes this possible through the sacrifice of his Son which is shown forth when the Last Supper is repeated. We can then only make a worthy offering because God has shown us the right way. So the Eucharist is entirely God's handiwork, even his private property, into which we are invited. This should be a warning about making human additions which would obscure God's masterpiece.

I should say finally that in writing this section I have been greatly helped by Tom Wright's *Jesus and the Victory of God*, pages 554–63.

Chapter 22:24–38.

After supper there is an anticlimax, when some of the disciples argue about who shall have the leading places in the kingdom. The flaws in those who have followed Jesus are clearly revealed, and he is under no illusions about them. He had called them to be spearheads in his revolutionary movement but knows that they are uncertain allies who may even pose a possible threat. They thought they were going to sit on actual physical thrones, and disputed who should get the most important one. Peter tried to stop Jesus going to his death, and Judas was about to betray him. Jesus could not trust even his closest associates. He now knows that he will go into the final battle alone, and needs to know if this is his Father's will. So he leads them out for a time of prayer.

Chapter 22:35–8. The swords.

These verses have caused problems to scholars. It has confirmed one in his idea that Jesus was a militant revolutionary – a para-Zealot. This is unlikely in view of the rest of Jesus' teaching, which was for peace and non-confrontation. Caird suggests that Jesus is comparing the first days of the disciples' mission in Galilee, when they could go out on their tours relying entirely on hospitality for their maintenance, with changed conditions when they will be in the hostile world. As a result of Jesus' treatment as a criminal, every man's hand will be against them. Jesus is using a metaphor but the disciples take it literally and he dismisses the subject: 'It is enough'.[54]

Chapter 22:39–46. Gethsemane.

In recent years pilgrims to the Holy Land have been conducted on a Maundy Thursday walk, following the steps of Our Lord and his disciples. They have met after dark in the Syrian Church where the institution of the Last Supper is read in Aramaic. Then they have walked through the streets to the Dung Gate; then, outside the city walls, they descended the rough slope to the Kedron Valley, across the dried-up stream into the garden of Gethsemane. Here they entered the modern church which covers some of the rocks of the garden, for prayer. With a large number of people, and stopping at intervals, the walk takes less than an hour. Jesus and his small band would have done it in less time.

Here Jesus knelt in desperate prayer, strengthened, as Luke notes, by an angel. The disciples fall asleep 'worn out by grief'.

Chapter 22:47–65. The arrest and High Priest's house.

The part played by Judas was essential because he both knew where Jesus could be found and also could identify him in the dark. It should be noted that the arrest was made by temple police for this was still a Jewish matter, and the Romans would not be involved until the morning. There was some kind of resistance, in which Jesus would have no part, and he healed the damaged ear of one of the arresting party. Jesus was then taken before the Jewish authorities. Luke alone says 'when day broke'. The other Gospels indicate that there was no delay, and that the confrontation took place immediately. This has posed difficulties for some scholars, who say that a trial by night was not allowed by Jewish law. However, if we accept that the real trial was held some weeks before, a second trial was not needed and Jesus had only to be confronted with the verdict and given a chance to refute it. This he could not do, but referred instead to Daniel's figure of the Son of Man, who had serious apocalyptic implications for the Jews, as we have seen earlier. This failed to satisfy the religious authorities, who saw no reason why a death sentence should not be carried out – for blasphemy. It remained only for Pilate to agree to an execution, but this had to wait until the morning. No Roman governor would leave his bed to satisfy a crowd of Jews!

Jesus could well have been kept in the dungeon in the High Priest's palace, which can still be seen among the ruins. It is a grim place into which a prisoner was lowered (see Jeremiah 38:6), and the words of Psalm 88, 'You have taken friend and neighbour far from me; darkness is my only companion', might well have been in Jesus' thoughts.

The Trials: Chapter 22:66 — 23:25.

Before the High Priest.

As has been noted already, there are difficulties in placing an actual trial immediately after Jesus' arrest as Matthew, Mark and John suggest. According to the Law trials had to be held in the daytime and in the Sanhedrin, the council chamber of Hewn Stones, so it would have been illegal to conduct the trial in the High Priest's palace. The night investigation was probably a way of establishing if Jesus accepted the authority of the High Priest, which he did not.

Luke says the trial took place in the morning, but there would scarcely have been time for this. It is therefore best to accept John's account of an earlier trial in Jesus' absence (11:47ff.).

Before Pilate.

There is now a race against time to have Jesus condemned to death before the Passover started. We have already noted that Pilate was in no mood to carry out the wishes of the Jews, for that would have been *lèse-majesté*, but in the end he had to submit to political blackmail. Perhaps to gain time he sent Jesus to Herod, as a piece of social etiquette.

Before Herod.

Jerusalem was a small city and official buildings were not far apart, so little time was wasted. We know that Herod was anxious to know more about Jesus. He might have been disappointed that he did not show the same fire as his cousin John Baptist. So he returned Jesus to Pilate for the last act of the drama, having treated him with contempt and made him a mock king.

The verdict.

Pilate now gives the people the choice of freeing either

Jesus or Barabbas, and the latter is chosen. Jesus is then sentenced to death by crucifixion.

The Crucifixion: Chapter 23:26–56.

This was a Roman method of execution and was designed to be the greatest possible deterrent to any who dared to defy Roman authority. Victims were stripped and flogged before being crucified in a public place. They then carried a wooden beam to the place of execution where it was placed across an upright post or tree. We are told that Simon, a man from Cyrene, was forced to carry this part of the cross. The reason for execution was sometimes displayed. In Jesus' case there might have been the Roman version, 'This is Jesus the King of the Jews', and a Jewish one which stated that Jesus was being put to death for blasphemy and sorcery.

Chapter 23:27ff. The women of Jerusalem.

We know how emotional Middle Eastern people can get at the sight of death, and here we have some women who give vent to their feelings. Jesus turns to them and warns of the coming disaster which will bring suffering to them and their children. Rather, says Our Lord, the woman who is barren will be considered lucky in those days. The Jews had chosen revolution and confrontation with Rome, and the youngsters playing in the streets would become the firebrands of the next generation and suffer terrible consequences. The women should save their tears for when they would be really needed. Jesus quotes words from Hosea 10:8 which describes the wickedness of the nation which would result in devastation.

So now Jesus had proclaimed divine judgement on Jerusalem, for her failure to repent, for her persistence in militant nationalism. This is not simply a matter of the Jewish leaders condemning him, and so pulling down upon their own heads a severe judgement in turn. It was a matter of the Romans condemning Jesus on a charge of which he was innocent and his compatriots guilty. He was the green tree, they the dry ... Jesus was now going ahead of the nation to undergo the punishment which, above all, symbolized the judgement on her rebel subjects. If they did this to a revolutionary who was not advocating rebellion against Rome, what would they do to those who were and those who followed them? (Wright).

Chapter 23:32ff.

They now came to a place called Golgotha or a Skull – was it because a skull could usually be found there, or because it was shaped like a skull? – which in those days was outside the city walls but in a later rebuilding was inside. (The sites of both the crucifixion and resurrection are now covered by the great Church of the Holy Sepulchre). Here the final acts of execution were carried out. The victims were stripped and hung from crosses. There has been some debate about whether nails were used, but in 1968 the bones of a man in his late twenties, who was crucified before AD 70, were found in an ossuary in Jerusalem. An iron nail was still in place through the right heel, and although the evidence is difficult to interpret, it suggests that his feet were nailed to either side of the upright stake. However it was done, crucifixion was a cruel method of execution, and a victim could hang for days until he finally died.

The forgiveness which Jesus came to bring the whole nation in his kingdom is now given again, as it had been to individuals during his ministry, and is now extended to the penitent criminal.

Darkness over the land.

There could not have been an eclipse of the sun at a time of a full moon, but the darkness and the rending of the curtain in the temple may well have been symbolic of the Day of the Lord which had been prophesied in the Old Testament (Joel 2:10).

Pilate and the penitent criminal had both declared Jesus

innocent. The centurion now adds his verdict, 'Truly this man was innocent'. So Luke explains to later readers the injustice of the Lord's death.

Chapter 23:49ff.

The Passover was about to begin, and it would have been against the Law to leave a dead body on the cross. So one of Jesus' followers, Joseph, organized a hurried burial in his own tomb. Round the base of the Holy Sepulchre Church traces of old tombs still remain, and excavation of actual tombs can be seen where in an inner chamber a bench has been hewn out of the rock for the body.

In the case of Jesus there was no time to anoint the body with spices – darkness was at hand and no Jew, especially women, would want to be outside the city after the Passover had started. So this work was left until the sabbath was over.

THE VICTORIOUS KINGDOM

The Resurrection: Chapter 24.

A new *Bible Handbook* sums up the importance of this final chapter.

> The belief that Jesus died on the cross and yet was alive after his death is the reason why the New Testament books were written and why Christianity exists. Although no one witnessed the Resurrection, the event is as real to the New Testament writers as the Crucifixion was. Apart from Mark's Gospel which has no post-resurrection appearance stories (the original Gospel stops at 16:8), the post-resurrection stories recorded in the other Gospels complement one another.[55]

There have been attempts in liberal theology to explain away what actually happened on the first Easter morning.

Some have argued that the spirit of Jesus was still alive, or that sheer grief gave people hallucinations, or that Jesus did not die on the cross but had fainted and then revived.

The evidence supports none of these theories. People were overwhelmed by the realization that Jesus was still alive and were even frightened by his appearances in bodily form. He clearly was the same Lord but in a different bodily form. In other words, he had not simply been revived but had died and risen again. The *Bible Handbook*, which is the work of many notable scholars, concludes that the fact of the resurrection is supported by four main areas of evidence: the reliability of the empty tomb tradition: the multiple witnesses to post-resurrection appearances which retain a note of total surprise: the experience of the early Church – its very existence being a major part of the evidence for the Resurrection: and an absence of satisfactory explanations.

Chapter 24:1–11. The women at the tomb.

As soon as possible after the sabbath, women followers came to complete the burial rites but found the stone rolled away and the sepulchre empty. They reported this to the disciples, who did not believe them.

Chapter 24:13ff. The Emmaus incident.

Two disciples were discussing the recent sad happening when they were joined by Jesus whom they did not recognize. Caird notes that the reason for this was that they were convinced that miracles of that kind could not happen. They still thought that he would be the Messiah of Jewish nationalist expectation, but Jesus rebuked them for not understanding Old Testament Scriptures, and perhaps also his own teaching about a different kingdom. God's purpose in creation was the formation of a special holy people dedicated to his service. This could only be achieved if that people was prepared to suffer. As the Old Testament shows, this suffering would happen in different ways, but triumph would come in the end, as the Suffering Servant passages in Isaiah prophesy.

All this Jesus teaches once again, and is finally recognized in the way he conducted the evening meal. He disappears, and they return to Jerusalem to tell the good news to others.

Chapter 24:36–end.

Jesus now gives proof to them all that he has truly risen from the dead, and repeats again the lessons of the Old Testament they should have learnt for themselves. The Gospel ends with the sending out on mission and the Ascension, which is the starting point of Luke's next book. '[Jesus] would bring Israel's history to its climax. Through his work, YHWH would defeat evil, bringing the kingdom to birth, and enable Israel to become after all, the light of the world.' (Wright).

POSTSCRIPT

PSALM 118:22: THE STONE WHICH THE BUILDERS REJECTED HAS BECOME THE CORNERSTONE

Throughout the Christian centuries there have been attempts to interpret what we have seen as Jewish events for later generations of believers. It would not be unfair to suggest that after the buoyant enthusiasm of the early Christians, the Catholic Church became more and more interested in what it meant for individuals within an increasingly organized movement. This became centred especially round the death and resurrection of Jesus. In early days it was essential for each believer to keep his contact with the risen Christ and develop an Easter Every Day spirituality. This included thanksgiving not only for the death of Jesus but also for his resurrection and ascension, and this was done within the Eucharist. In all of Our Lord's works believers could see the love of God at work, expressed beautifully by John in his First Letter: This is what love really is: not that we have loved God but that he loved us and sent his Son as a sacrifice to atone for our sins (1 John 4:10).

So, what God has done for us in Christ's death and resurrection should make us love him, love in exchange for love. This is probably the simplest interpretation which Christians through the ages have put on Holy Week and Easter.

In John's letter, however, there is the idea of sacrifice
and atonement for sins, and this too has been developed
by the Church. Very quickly, as the Letter to the Hebrews
shows, the focus of a Christian worshipper was trans-
ferred from an earthly temple in Jerusalem to the great
high priest who has entered the heavens and continually
offers himself to the Father on our behalf. We may join in
this sacrifice both as family and as individuals. We sing
today an English version of an old Greek hymn:

> His Manhood pleads where now it lives
>   On heaven's eternal throne
> And where in mystic rite he gives
>   Its presence to his own
>
> And so we show thy death, O Lord,
>   Till thou again appear,
> And feel, when we approach thy board
>   We have an altar here.

The enthusiasm of the first Christians changed when
the Church spread rapidly and standards began to drop. A
sense of *non sum dignus*, unworthiness, began to creep in,
which increased as people joined the Church as a matter of
course or routine. The idea of Jesus dying for our sins,
making atonement, took over. As the modern hymn says:

> There was no other good enough
>   To pay the price of sin;
> He only could unlock the gate
>   Of heaven, and let us in.

At times, such developments have been taken to
extremes in both Catholic and Protestant directions. The
Mass has become a repeat of Calvary without a celebration
of the Lord's subsequent triumphant resurrection, and
there have been attempts to gain salvation by extreme
mortification. In Protestant terms the death of Jesus has

been like a cloak thrown over a converted sinner to turn away the wrath of God. Christians generally have slipped into a religious life which is more concerned with personal reward and gaining heaven than with creating a loving community.

We might therefore return to the gospel to find out how Jesus viewed his earthly ministry and teaching. He certainly saw himself as coming to his own nation to demand what was owing to his Father in terms of daily living. This is clearly seen in the parable of the wicked tenants where the vinegrowers refused to give the owner his rightful due. When the son comes he is killed and thrown out of the vineyard. It is here that Jesus adds the quotation from Psalm 118: 'the stone which the builders rejected has become the chief cornerstone'. This follows the previous cleansing of the temple, when for a brief spell the temple system is suspended because money cannot be changed and animals for sacrifice cannot be bought. There is little doubt that this was meant to be a foretaste of the final destruction of the temple forty years later. However, as we learn from John 2:19ff. Jesus would provide a replacement centre of worship in his own body. 'Destroy this temple and in three days I will raise it up again', and John in the light of the Lord's resurrection adds, 'But the temple he was speaking of was his body'. Later, in his conversation with the Samaritan woman at Jacob's well, he could indicate that neither on Mount Gerizim nor in Jerusalem would God be worshipped.

So after his death and resurrection Jesus as the Son of Man took his wounded yet victorious body to his Father, the Ancient of Days, and was given sovereignty, glory and kingly power as Daniel had prophesied. But he remained the cornerstone of a new temple, not made with hands but with his own person, and his followers must build upon that foundation. St Peter's commentary on this rebuilding teaches how this must happen: 'He is the living stone, rejected by men but chosen by God and precious to him: set yourselves close to him so that you, too, the holy priesthood that offers the spiritual sacrifices which Jesus made acceptable to God, may be living stones making a spiritual house' (1 Peter 2:4ff.). Here we have the full picture of what Jesus has done for his people and how they may build upon his work. There can be little doubt that this was the substance of his final instruction to his disciples between his resurrection and ascension. He did not have to give new teaching but merely remind them of what he had taught them in the Sermon on the Plain, at Bethsaida on the shore of Galilee, and elsewhere. It will be the poor in spirit, the loving, the gentle and humble, who will form the new kingdom of God. If we add to this John's version of Jesus' teaching where the emphasis is on love for the other, then we have the essential ingredients for the formation of 'living stones'. So the followers of Jesus had to be remoulded and then go out to find more bricks for a church which would never be finished until the end of time.

The success of these final briefings could be seen in the loving communities which came into being after Pentecost, which no doubt prompted Luke to investigate their origin. The 'living stones' by their life style attracted many, and this has remained the lesson for Christians in every generation up to today.

REFERENCES

1. *Another Look at St John's Gospel* (Church Literature Association, 1990)
2. Newsome, *The Victorian World Picture* (Murray, 1997), p. 195
3. Schleiermacher trans. Thirlwall.
4. Hastings, A., *A History of English Christianity 1920–1985* (Collins, 1986)
5. ibid., pp. 649f.
6. Chapman, 1967 (under Revelation)
7. Moule, C.F.D. *The Phenomenon of the New Testament* (SCM, 1967), pp. 79 and 113
8. Thucydides, *Peloponnessian War* (Loeb) Ch XXII
9. Newsome, op. cit.
10. Gracewing, 1996.
11. Cambridge, 1984, p. 11f.
12. op. cit., pp. 702–3 notes 3–4.
13. SCM, 1976.
14. Hastings, op. cit., p. 652
15. SCM, 1985.
16. SPCK, 1996.
17. Brown, R., *Introduction to the New Testament* (Doubleday, 1997), p. 226
18. Robinson, J.A.T., *Redating the New Testament* (SCM, 1976), p. 10
19. Brown, op. cit., p. 226
20. Moule, op. cit., p. 113

21. Wright, N.T., *Jesus and the Victory of God* (SPCK, 1996), p. 104
22. Bockmuehl, M., *This Jesus* (T&T Clark, 1994), p. 122
23. Bockmuehl, op. cit., p. 34
24. Caird, G.B., *St Luke* (Pelican, 1963), p. 47
25. Caird, op. cit., p. 55
26 Brown, op. cit., p. 235.
27. Caird, op. cit., p. 81
28. Wright, op. cit., p. 461
29. Wright, op. cit., p. 300
30. Wright, op. cit., pp. 287ff.
31. Wright, op. cit., p. 450
32. Caird, op. cit., p. 81
33. Moule, op. cit., p. 63ff.
34. Wright, op. cit., pp. 230ff.
35. Wright, op. cit., p. 196
36. Brown, op. cit., p. 242
37. Wright, op. cit., Ch. 7
38. Wright, op. cit., p. 298
39. Caird, op. cit., p. 132
40 Wright, op. cit., p. 307
41. Wright, op. cit., pp. 229ff.
42. Jeremias, *Rediscovering the Parables* (SCM, 1966), p. 106
43. Wright, op. cit., p. 127
44. Caird, op. cit., p. 186
45. Jeremias, op. cit., p. 144
46. Wright, op. cit., p. 260
47. Wright, op. cit., pp. 343ff.
48. Caird, op. cit., p. 209
49. Sanders, E.P., *The Historical Figure of Jesus* (Lane, 1993), p. 27

50. Wright, op. cit., pp. 497ff.
51. Wright, op. cit., p. 508
52. Bowker, John (ed.) *The Complete Bible Handbook* (Dorling Kindersley, 1998), p. 263
53. Robinson, John, *The Priority of John* (SCM, 1985), pp. 263ff.
54. Caird, op. cit., p. 240
55. *The Complete Bible Handbook*, op. cit., p. 364

BIBLIOGRAPHY

Bowker, John (ed.), *The Complete Bible Handbook*, Dorling Kindersley, 1998

Bockmuehl, M., *This Jesus*, Edinburgh, T&T Clark, 1994

Brown, Raymond, *An Introduction to the New Testament*, New York, Doubleday, 1997

Caird, G.B., *St Luke*, London, Pelican, 1963

Clutterbuck, H.I., *A Church in Miniature*, Leominster, Gracewing, 1995

Hastings, Adrian, *A History of English Christianity 1920–1985*, London, Collins, 1986

Jeremias, *Rediscovering the Parables*, SCM, 1996

Moule, C.F.D., *Phenomenon of the New Testament*, London, SCM, 1961

Newsome, *The Victorian World Picture*, London, Murray, 1997

Robinson, J.A.T., *The Priority of John*, SCM, 1985

Robinson, J.A.T., *Redating the New Testament*, SCM, 1976

Wright, N.T., *Jesus and the Victory of God*, London, SPCK, 1996

Printed in the United Kingdom
by Lightning Source UK Ltd.
120002UK00001B/97